THE BARGE COAST
of
SUFFOLK, ESSEX AND KENT

ROBERT SIMPER

Vol 4 The Coast in the Past Series
ROBERT SIMPER

Published by Creekside Publishing 2007
www.creeksidepublishing.co.uk

ISBN 0-9538506-8-4
978-0-9538506-8-6

Printed by Lavenham Press Ltd, Lavenham, Suffolk

Front cover: The bowsprit barge *Xylonite* in the Lower Hope at the start of the Thames Sailing Barge Match, 2001.
Back cover: [top] The *Victor* and *Repertor* in the Pin Mill Sailing Barge Match, 2007.
[bottom]The *Two Belles* and *Dorothy* on Aldeburgh beach. 2005.

Books by the same author:-

EAST ANGLIAN BOOKS
Over Snape Bridge (1967)
Woodbridge & Beyond (1972)
Suffolk Show (1981)
East Anglian Coast & Waterways (1985)
Suffolk Sandlings (1986)
Woodbridge: A Pictorial History (1995)
Suffolk: A Fine Farming County (2007)

SAIL BOOKS
East Coast Sail (1972)
Scottish Sail (1974)
North East Sail (1975)
British Sail (1977)
Victorian & Edwardian Yachting from Old Photographs (1978)
Gaff Sail (1979)
Sail on the Orwell (1982)
Sail: The Surviving Tradition (1984)

BRITISH ISLES
Britain's Maritime Heritage (1982)
Beach Boats of Britain (1984)

ENGLISH ESTUARIES SERIES
The River Deben (1992)
The River Orwell and the River Stour (1993)
Rivers Alde, Ore and Blyth (1994)
Essex Rivers and Creeks (1995)
Norfolk Rivers and Harbours (1996)
Thames Tideway (1997)
River Medway and The Swale (1998)
Rivers to the Fens (2000)
Up the River Deben (2006)

AUTOBIOGRAPHICAL
In Search of Sail (1998)
Family Fields (1999)
Voyage Around East Anglia (2001)
Creekside Tales (2004)

COAST IN THE PAST SERIES
Forgotten Coast (2002)   British Isles
Sunrise Coast (2002)   Suffolk & N.Essex
The Lugger Coast (2003)   Cornwall & Devon

Whitstable smack *Thistle* in the River Orwell 2007.

'Evening on the River Blackwater' by Roger Finch.

CONTENTS

The coasting barge *Lady Daphne* was built in 1923 and could load 220 tons. She is seen here going under Tower Bridge, London. Tower Bridge crosses the Pool of London, where Queenhithe was the centre of the original port of London.

RECORDING THE LIVING TRADITION

The Thames sailing barge is the icon of the East Coast, while the smacks and other former workboats are not so well known outside their home areas. However they are all part of the past and the future of this coast. The traditional boats are at the heart of the local identity, fuelled by nostalgia and their functional beauty, many people battle to keep them going.

Providing you understood their limitations, the East Coast workboats were highly effective. The Golden Age of working sail on the coast of Britain was just before World War I. This was the peak of centuries of trial and error. It started with the Anglo-Saxons, with open clinker longships, and slowly over the centuries improvements were made. However, seafaring men were highly suspicious of change. They were cautious of going to sea in a new type of boat because they risked their lives. If they failed to return then their families were often left to starve and they were worried about their dependants. However, there were always some enterprising men ready to try something new if it failed, such as the Victorian fashion for snib bow smacks, then it was quickly forgotten. If a new hull shape or rig was seen to be an improvement, then everybody wanted one. The practical working boats were more than just working tools. These boats were the centre of the lives of the people in coastal communities and were the source of great pride to their owners and crews.

I have spent a lifetime sailing on these craft, and am just starting to understand them, but to make this record I have drawn on a wide range of sources. The owners and crews, past and present, undoubtedly gave the greatest insight into these boats. Starting at the beginning, Michael Rowe at the River and Rowing Museum, Henley-on-Thames, allowed me to photograph their excellent West Country barge model. Tony Winter lent the photograph of *Lord Roberts*, the barge he rigged out in 1964 after she had been a motor barge.

Barry Pearce has a superb knowledge of the barge era and, most importantly, read through and improved the rough draft of this work. Barry made his first trip on a sailing barge in about 1954 when he should have been at Camberwell School of Art, but instead more enjoyed the company of Bob Roberts, his mate and dog aboard the *Cambria*. He went on to be a barge mate and skipper and then ran the W.Cook & Son barge yard at Maldon.

Janet Harker has drawn the maps and illustrations and organized GGS Creative Graphics to bring the faded oyster skiff plan back to life. Janet first visited Maldon when she was at school and after attending the Royal College of Art came back to teach sailing at the Maldon Youth Hostel. It was in the late 1950s that she saw the last of the smacks sailing down river and became intrigued with the world they belonged too. Maldon, like most places along the coast, had the old communities of seafarers whose lives revolved around the local workboats. It was in those years that Janet took the photograph of Alfa Pitt (Chapter Four).

Tony Smith has allowed me to use the plans of the *Venta*, lines that he actually took from the barge in 1964. Nat Wilson of the International Boatbuilding Training Centre, Lowestoft had the lines taken off the Woodbridge pilot's skiff *Teddy* and has allowed me to use them here.

Perhaps very special thanks should go to Frank Knights of Woodbridge, always helpful with information on the past, but in this case he kept the Woodbridge pilot's boat *Teddy* in a shed for over fifty years. This unique example of a Victorian rowing skiff has survived into modern times when many such boats were simply broken up or burnt.

Around the coast information has come from Clive 'Brom' Bromley, Trevor Osborne and Steve Meddle at Leigh-on-Sea, Tim Goldsack of Faversham, Gerard Swift of West Mersea, and Steve Hall of Wivenhoe and Tollesbury. On barges in trade thanks to Jim Lawrence and Pat Fisher.

Tony Robinson was working at the shipyard of James & Stone, Brightlingsea when they closed and he rescued the plans of the *Millie*, *Sarah* and oyster skiff from the office before they were destroyed. These were badly faded, but I thought they were of such interest that they should be copied and made available to the public.

At Shingle Street both Tim Miller and Nina Harris talked about their very different family memories that stretched way back into the nineteenth century. In 1975 I met the ninety-year-old Thorpeness fisherman Harry Harling in his cottage, where he had lived all his life. This cottage, now surrounded by houses, once stood on the open sand dunes when his great grandfather had it built in the late eighteenth century. Thirty-two years later I returned to meet his grandson John Harling in the same cottage, and it had hardly changed. In those three decades Aldeburgh's fleet of boats fishing off the beach has gone from the most successful beach landing in East Anglia down to the verge of extinction. If there are fewer fish out there to be caught then there are fewer boats on the beach.

My wife Pearl helped with the editing, and took some of the photographs, but I took most of the others. Fortunately Diana McMillan returned from more ocean voyaging in time to do the main editing.

In theory the working sailing craft were built in feet and inches, but most wooden craft were actually built by eye, often from a half model, and then measured up afterwards for registration. Most of the wooden barges are actually slightly different on either side. Some are reputed to sail better on one tack than the other. The steel barges were built from plans but they were not necessarily better sailers.

The idea of quoting measurements is to give some idea of the size of each craft, but frankly this is fraught with difficulty because different sources quote different dimensions. It is worth mentioning that one foot(ft) is 60cm while one meter is 3.28ft. The measurements given here are from stem to stern, the maximum beam and depth of the sides at the lowest point. In some cases just the draft, the amount of water drawn aft, is quoted.

RS.
Ramsholt 2007.

Chapter One

BUILT FOR A PURPOSE
Around the barge ports

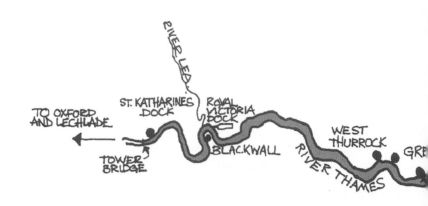

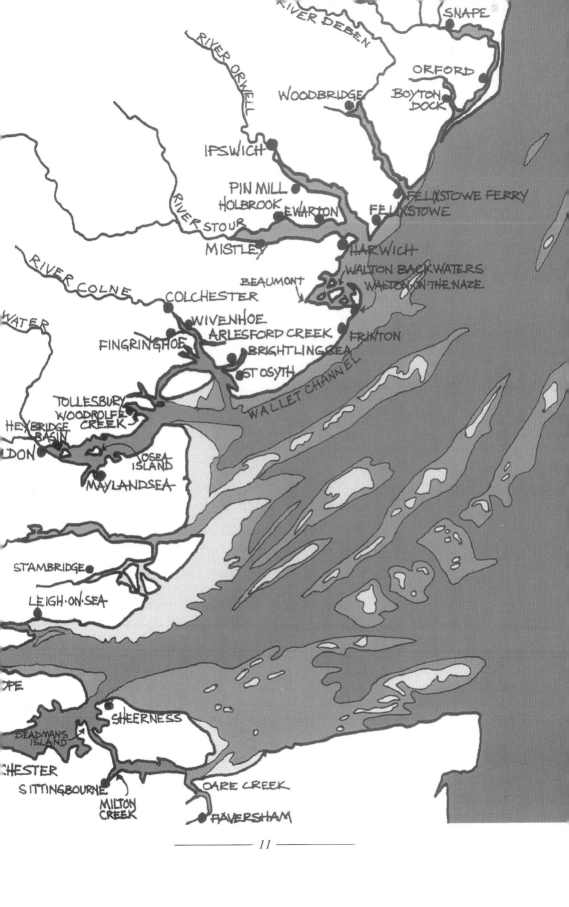

The model of the 1820 West Country barge *Good Intent* in the River and Rowing Museum, Henley-on-Thames. The West Country barges carried goods from the Pool of London up the fresh water Thames to Oxford and on to Lechlade. These barges loaded up to 200 tons on a 4ft draft and used a square sail or were rowed, poled or hauled up river.

The early flat-bottom barges on the inland Thames were clinker built (over- lapping planks), a type of craft evolved from the Anglo-Saxon and Viking ships. As it was difficult to build large hulls with a clinker method, flat-sided, flat-bottomed carvel hull (plank on end) barges appeared at the end of the 1600s. These flat-bottomed West Country barges were cheaper to build and had flat sloping 'swim head' bows. The sloping bow funnelled water under the hull and lifted it out of the water. To reduce the draft by even a few inches was a great advantage when operating in shallow waters.

The barges working on the Thames tideway were a very English craft that evolved by experimenting with different rigs and hulls. The great boxy hulls of the West Country barges were so easy and cheap to build that a smaller version was built for the tideway and with a spritsail rig and leeboard this proved very effective. The researches of Hugh Perks and Dr Robin Craig suggest that the first recorded Thames sailing barge, which was not a West Country barge or sailing lighter, was the *Edward and Mary* built at Chelsea in 1753. Typical of these early sailing barges was the 55.9 x 16.5 x 5.10ft *Albion* built at Limehouse in 1785. By the end of the eighteenth century sailing barges were being built and owned in Essex and Kent and not long afterwards in Suffolk, but they retained the name Thames Barges.

Sailing barges were built to earn money for their owners and crews and the freight market on the Thames and adjoining East Coast became highly competitive. The vast number of barges built allowed many new ideas to be tried and highly effective sailing craft evolved.

The swim head barge *Fertile* anchored in the River Colne. The *Fertile* was built in 1936 of Swedish rolled iron as a London River 'dumb' towing barge for the lightering trade. She had been rescued from a scrapyard to become a houseboat and was rigged out to sail by Steve Brotherhood. The *Fertile* gives an impression of the early spritsail barges.

The *Lady of the Lea*, built as a stumpie in 1931 to carry explosives from Waltham Abbey on the River Lea. The *Lady of the Lea* is a complete throwback in design to the earliest tiller steered barges on the Thames.

The stumpie barge *Nellie* off Mayland Creek. The *Nellie* was built in 1901 as a stays'l barge with a topmast and became a houseboat at Twickenham and later moved to Maldon. Because she does not have a topmast she is classified as a 'stumpie.'

The spritsail rig, which was common all over northern Europe, allowed the sails to be controlled very quickly. This was important when sailing in narrow channels, although the key factor was the leeboards which, when lowered, gripped the water and allowed the barges to sail against the wind. In the Victorian era the great breakthrough was the fitting of winches to handle the sails and leeboards. Larger barges could then be built, but still be handled by two men. The Thames barges' great secret of success was that they could sail light, without a cargo, and didn't need ballast. Because they only drew a few feet of water they could get into shallow creeks as well as make passages in the open sea.

Most rivers had small barges that just worked within the estuaries. The tiller-steered *Cygnet* was built in 1881 for the Ewarton farmer Walter Wrinch and carried small freights of wheat from the farm wharves on the rivers Stour, Orwell and Deben to the mills at Felixstowe Dock and Ipswich Dock. The *Cygnet's* mast is stepped well forward because she has a single hatch.

The barge *Victor*, built at Ipswich in 1895, rounding the NE Eagle buoy.

The steel barge *Wyvenhoe*, built Wivenhoe in 1896, off Colne Point.

The 'sprittie barges', *Cabby* and *Alice* in the Royal Victoria Dock with the new London Dockland buildings rising up in the background. At its height the Port of London had 30 miles of wharves and 1000 vessels a week arriving, making it the largest port in the world. When ships discharged 'overside' into barges, while at anchor in the Pool of London, they didn't pay any dock dues. In the docks when cargoes were discharged straight over the side into barges they were also free of dock charges and in order to save money merchants used barges whenever possible. This encouraged the use of both sailing and dumb barges.

The *Cabby*, built in Rochester at Gill's Lower Yard in 1928, was the last full-size wooden barge built. She could load 160 tons to sea and 180 tons in the river. As the London & Rochester Trading Company were a 'seeking' firm competing for general cargo they converted their craft to motor barges sooner than most. The London & Rochester progressed to a fleet of coastal power craft, but after the name changed to Crescent Shipping the *Cabby* was rigged out again as their promotion barge.

The *Alice* was a swim-head dumb barge, built in 1954 to load 115 tons. Owen and Rita Emerson fitted a bow and stern on the *Alice* at Upnor and she began sailing as a spritsail barge in 1997.

The steel barge *Portlight* in the Lower Hope, at the mouth of the London River in 1996. The *Portlight* shows the strong influence of racing on the remaining barges. She has a larger sail area than she had in trade. A working crew of two seldom used a pole for booming out a sail and the leeboards are the larger steel type that Alan Reekie pioneered for racing in the late 1970s on the *Ironsides*.

The *May* approaching the Mid Swatch buoy, the turning mark in the shortened course of the Thames Sailing Barge Match, 2001. The Jenkin Swatch is a channel for small vessels that links the Thames and the Medway.
   The tradition of racing is very strong in the barge world. Bargemen raced for cargoes, the first barge past an agreed mark got the next cargo and there were spasmodic local regatta races in the early nineteenth century. In 1863 Henry Dodd organized the first Thames Sailing Barge Match. Although the Thames and Medway races were only held once a year and only a few barges took part, they had a considerable effect on barge design. Owners started to build barges just to win these prestigious events. The Thames Sailing Barge Match claims to be the world's second oldest sailing event, after the America's Cup.

Tim Goldsack's steel barge *Decima* off Southend. *Decima* was built by Fay, at Southampton in 1899 for E.J. & W. Goldsmith whose head office was in Fenchurch Street, but their barge yard was at Grays in Essex.

In the 1890s the London barge owner Edward Goldsmith started an aggressive business campaign to take over the more lucrative East Coast trades. Goldsmiths steel barges were built quickly and cheaply and were intended to load more tons per crew member than their competitors. The Goldsmith barges were standardized into classes so that sails and fittings could be interchanged, which prevented them from having to wait for spares.

The construction of Goldsmith's steel barges started in 1898 when they ordered twenty-nine barges intended to load 150 tons with a crew of two. *Decima* and *Melissa* were amongst those built at Southampton with round chines (where the sides meets the bottom), but these proved difficult to sail light (without cargo) and their crews didn't like going to sea with more than 130 tons. However the batch built on the Thames had square chines, were much better sailers and loaded 150 tons.

Goldsmith's class of 85ft x 21ft 6ins x 6ft 4ins barges which could load 180 tons were built, but their *IC* class, built in around 1903, were 90ft x 23ft 2ins x 9ft and could load 240 tons to sea and 280 tons in the rivers. These were by far the largest spritsail barges then trading.

To finance the rapid growth of the Goldsmith brothers fleet they mortgaged a barge as soon as it was launched and this raised the capital to pay for the next craft. Goldsmiths competitive approach led to them hauling much of the material for the construction of the huge Moles at Dover Harbour, but they were blamed for bringing down the freight rate of paper between Snodland and London. A report of a bargemen's protest meeting recorded that some bargemen called Edward Goldsmith a 'mean old humbug' and that was probably only the polite version.

By 1905 Goldsmiths had a fleet of 147 barges and were dominating the barge trade from the London River. This was really the golden age of Thames spritsail barges because in around 1910 there was a downturn in coastal trade. Jim Lawrence remembers, in about 1948, Goldsmith's remaining barges were lying off Grays with their crews, many of whom were elderly and had been with the firm all their lives, waiting for orders to load a cargo, which never came. In 1949 Goldsmiths sold eleven of their barges to the London & Rochester Trading Co. and soon afterwards their last barges, *Briton* and *Scot*, were sold.

In 2006 only *Decima* and *Melissa* remained active barges, but in the 1990s both were given square chines. Another Fay-built barge, the *Scotia*, is abandoned in a creek opposite the Hythe Quay, Maldon. The 90ft *Celtic* was abandoned at the defunct Dolphin Barge Museum, Sittingbourne and the 89 x 21ft *Trojan* was abandoned in Leigh Creek.

Two 'cocklers' at Old Leigh, Leigh on Sea with a view over the mud flats towards the Thames mouth. The flat bottomed, shallow-draught barges were evolved to work into this type of creek.

A narrow gut of a channel leads up to Old Leigh, but sailing barges didn't attempt to go up the channel; they only took cargoes to Leigh on the spring tides and then sailed over the top of the mudflats. When motors were fitted barges started coming up the creek channel on neap tides, but some, like the *Clara*, got stuck across the channel and twisted their hulls badly.

The stem of the barge *Eve Annie* can just be seen in the background. She was the last tiller-steered 'stackie' that traded until about 1933.

Benjamin and Charles Cremer put up the Big Shed, on the point where Oare Creek joins up with Faversham Creek. They built barges here to ship their brick to London. The barge *Nellie* was built here in 1901.

Since Barry Tester and his son Dan took over the old Cremer yard they have totally rebuilt the smacks *Primrose*, *Lily May*, *Ethel Ada*, *Alberta* and *Harriet Blanche*. In the centre is the *Alberta* that has a very tall mast for racing.

The 36ft bawley *Thistle* at Tester's Yard on Oare Creek. The *Thistle* was built at Rochester in 1887 but was later owned by Bill Sunderland at Gravesend and, until she was sold in 1970, was the last bawley kept at Bawley Bay, Gravesend. Philip Wilkinson rebuilt this bawley between 1976-81.

The sailing barges *Henry*, *Lady of the Lea*, *Repertor* and *Decima* seen at the Standard Quay, Faversham. There were very determined attempts to keep the commercial port of Faversham open, but in the end shipping simply grew too large to get up here and the last cargo was delivered in 1989. In 1992 some barge owners and local people started to develop Standard Quay as a traditional boat centre. Pollock's shipyard across the creek was developed for housing and in 2004 a property developer tried to build housing on Standard Quay, but this was vigorously fought off.

One of the last cargoes taken by a sailing barge to Standard Quay was canned pineapple by the *Portlight* in about 1955. Skipper Gordon Hardy remarked later 'It was a bit of a tragedy when we went there, one of cases got dropped on the quay. We were eating pineapple for months afterwards'

Peter Dodds' barge *Mirosa* at the Iron Bridge Wharf, Faversham. The *Mirosa* was built in 1892 by John Howard at Maldon. Howard was noted for building attractive fast sailing barges, smacks and yachts, between 1879-1912. The *Mirosa* was launched at 2pm on June 28 and on her hundredth birthday she returned to Maldon under sail. On her hundred and fifteenth birthday she did a charter trip up the Swale, and because of strong winds sailed up over The Grounds, to Ridham Dock. This barge has paid her way without an engine.

When passage making the flat-bottomed barges didn't usually sail against the tide in the Thames Estuary, but were anchored to wait for a 'fair' tide in their favour. In bad weather barges sheltered, 'windbound,' in such anchorages as the Stone Heaps in the Orwell, Pyefleet in the Colne, the mouth of the Crouch, mouth of the Medway and the Lower Hope in the Thames.

In fine weather they anchored wherever the tide turned against them. In February 1955 the *May* and *Portlight*, bound for the Thames, anchored in the Wallet when the weather turned bad. The next day the Walton and Clacton lifeboats had to help them recover their anchors and tow them back into Harwich.

Since they never knew how long a passage under sail would take, days or weeks, the bargemen's whole life was totally unpredictable. Roger Edmonds, who lived on a houseboat at Woodbridge, but had been a Cranfields skipper, summed it up with saying 'bargemen never make plans.'

Overleaf: Geoff 'Frog' Ingle's barge *Orinoco* being fitted out at the Iron Bridge Wharf, Faversham.

After being built at East Greenwich in 1895 the *Orinoco was* bought by Mason, who owned the cement works at Waldringfield. Mason lived in a large house on the seafront at Felixstowe and used to watch out for his barges returning from the Thames. He had a white circle emblem put in their tops'ls so that he could identify all of them.

In 1988 eighty-two year old Deben pilot Billy Newson told me that his father Charlie, also a Deben pilot, had once seen fourteen sailing barges appear off the Deben Bar all ready to come in on one tide. The owners always had great difficulty in knowing the whereabouts of their barges as the skippers sailed off and often didn't turn up at the next port for weeks. When Mason sold his barges to Cranfield Bros. they kept the white circle in their tops'ls and R. & W. Paul then decided they would put a 'X' in their barges tops'ls. It was not unknown for someone in Paul's office, in Ipswich, to be sent off to Shotley on the bus to see if any of their barges were laying at anchor in Harwich Harbour.

The sheer number of barges that were once sailing takes some believing now. In Kent, Milton Creek, up to Sittingbourne, was only two miles long, but there were several cement works and old Kent bargemen claimed to have seen as many as sixty barges leaving this tiny creek on a single tide.

The 44ft Colchester smack *Ellen* and the barge *Greta* in Whitstable Harbour. The *Ellen*, built by Harris at Rowhedge in 1900, is known as the 'Three Swans' because her number is *CK222*. The *Greta* was built in 1892, by Stone, at Brightlingsea. The *Greta* was originally one of the Howe's of Colchester barges that had black top-s'ls.

Barges at the Hythe, Maldon after the Blackwater Sailing Barge Match in 2005. Maldon, a typical barge port that dries out at low tide, has become a centre of sailing barge activity, but in the working era it was simply one of many similar country ports. Because it was inexpensive to hire a berth at the Hythe, barges that had been bought for pleasure sailing and charter work started to gather here in the early 1960's.

Plans of the *Venta*, a coasting barge built by Howard at Maldon in 1893. These plans were drawn by Tony Smith just before the *Venta*, owned by Jocelyn Lukins, was sailed without an engine from Maldon to Sweden and back by skipper John Fairbrother. This barge was destroyed by fire at Cuxton in 1991.

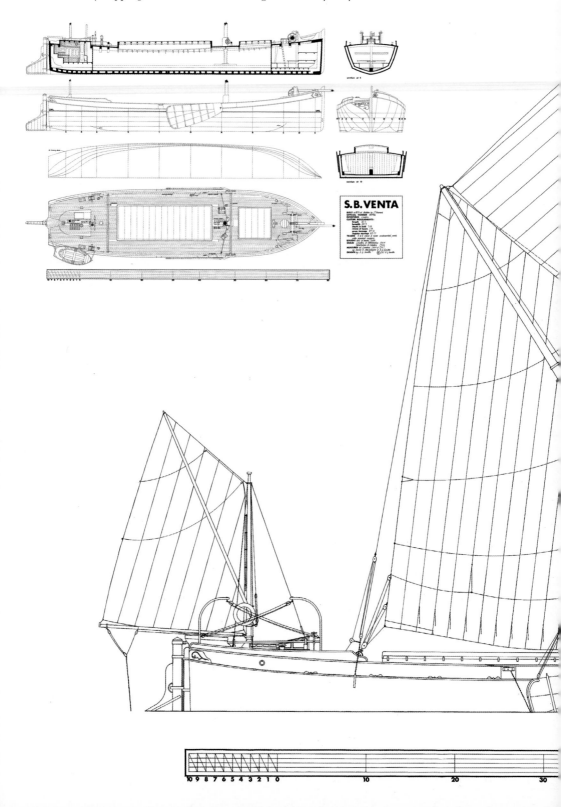

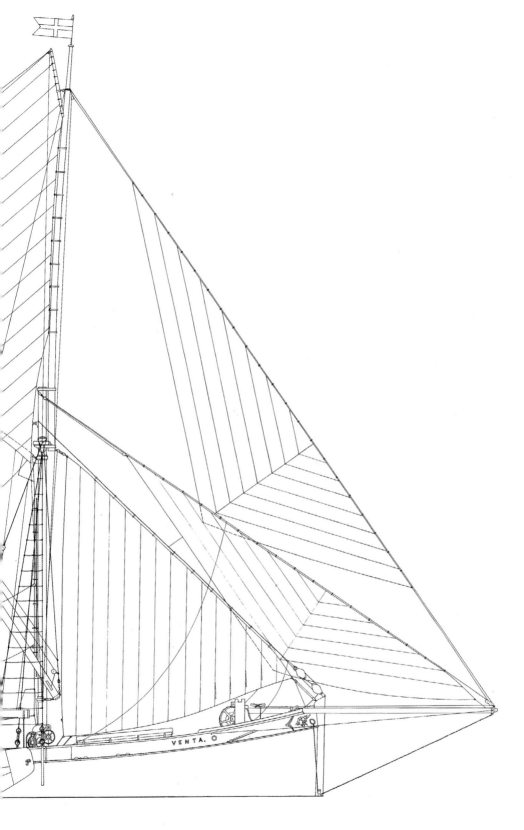

50   60   70   80

S.B. VENTA

© 1967 A.G. Smith

The steel barges *Xylonite* and *Portlight* and the wooden barge *Gladys* at Fullbridge, Maldon.

The Granary at Woodrolfe Creek, Tollesbury was built on stilts in about 1865. Goods were originally discharged at Old Hall, at the head of Tollesbury Creek, but after the Granary was built barges came up Woodrolfe Creek. This creek's name is a corruption of 'wood up' because timber ships also came in here. The farm at the head of the creek was also shown on ancient maps as 'Wood-Up.'

Ruben Chappell's ship's portrait of the *Mary & Kate*, built at Blackwall in 1890 for George Walker and Thomas Howard's English and Continental Shipping. In the 1890s Walker and Howard of Mark Lane, London built up their fleet of wooden coasting 'boomie' gaff-rigged barges. The largest of their fifteen *Lord* barges was the *Lord Alcester* that loaded 290 tons.

In about 1905 the Walker & Howard fleet were sold up and *Mary and Kate* was bought by Will Frost of Tollesbury and she traded with coal up to Woodrolfe Creek. When Frost owned *Mary and Kate* she had a sprit-sail mainsail, to cut down the number of hands needed, but retained a gaff mizzen, two jibs on a fixed bowsprit and carried her boat on the hatches in true coaster fashion. She was one of the many barges that vanished in the inter-war trade 'slump,' although by about 1932 she was owned by Charles Dines, of Gravesend.

"Lord Roberts" heading West in Royal Victoria Dock.

The *Lord Roberts* working up the Royal Victoria Dock, London with skipper Tom White at the tiller. The *Lord Roberts* was built by Cook & Woodward at Maldon in 1900 and spent most of her career, with *Joy*, taking imported wheat from London docks to the mill at Stambridge on the River Roach.

From the early 1870s most barges had wheel steering so the *Lord Roberts* was probably the last full-size barge built with tiller steering. The stackie barges kept tiller steering because the response was quicker when working up creeks. If a barge grounded in an uneven spot and the rudder lifted there was no steering gear to get damaged. However a tiller, known as 'a rib tickler,' had been known to break ribs and throw men overboard, even with tackles used on both sides. Most skippers liked a wheel better because in cold weather they could stand down on the cabin steps, and get some of the heat from the cabin fire, and just steer with the bottom spoke of the wheel.

The *Dawn* in about 1924, before she was 'doubled' with an extra layer of planks, at Fullbridge, Maldon near Green's Mill. Shortly after this the *Dawn* was sold to Francis & Gilders of Colchester and became a 'seeking' barge that took any cargo they could get. Henry Howes' barges, with their black tops'ls, had been the main Colchester 'seeking' barges, but in 1915 his nephew Joshua Francis started to get a fleet of 'seeking' barges together. Francis teamed up with the London freight broker Cecil Gilders to form Francis & Gilders which in about 1952 became part of the London & Rochester Trading Co. who took over most of the remaining 'seeking' barges in the Thames Estuary.

Francis & Gilders kept their smaller barges to work wheat up under Hythe Bridge to Marriage's East Mills, but when this trade finished they were sold to Brown & Son and were used as lighters to bring timber from ships at Osea Island up to Heybridge Basin, where it was taken by canal to Chelmsford. During 1955 Francis & Gilders' last sailing barges, *Mirosa, George Smeed, Centaur* and *Kitty*, were stripped of their gear at Colchester and sold to become timber lighters at Heybridge Basin. As *Dawn* had a low-powered engine she traded until about 1960 and then also went to Heybridge Basin as a lighter.

Francis & Gilders' manager, Headley Farrington, thought that sailing barges were finished so he had all the remaining sails, spars, blocks, and the *Dawn's* old tiller with its yellow lettering, cleared out of the sheds at their yard and burnt. A few years later the era of people buying barge hulls to rig out began and people went to Headley desperate to buy old gear. 'We could have made a fortune!' Headley commented sadly.

The wooden *Phoenician*, built in 1922, steel *Repertor* and the *Reminder* at the start of the Maldon Barge Match off Osea Island, 2007.

The abandoned sand-loading jetty in Alresford Creek. It seems that this jetty was first used in 1932 and barge traffic finished in 1958. Before 1914 stackie barges loaded on The Ford across the creek and on five places between here and the dock at Thorrington Tide Mill at the head of the creek.

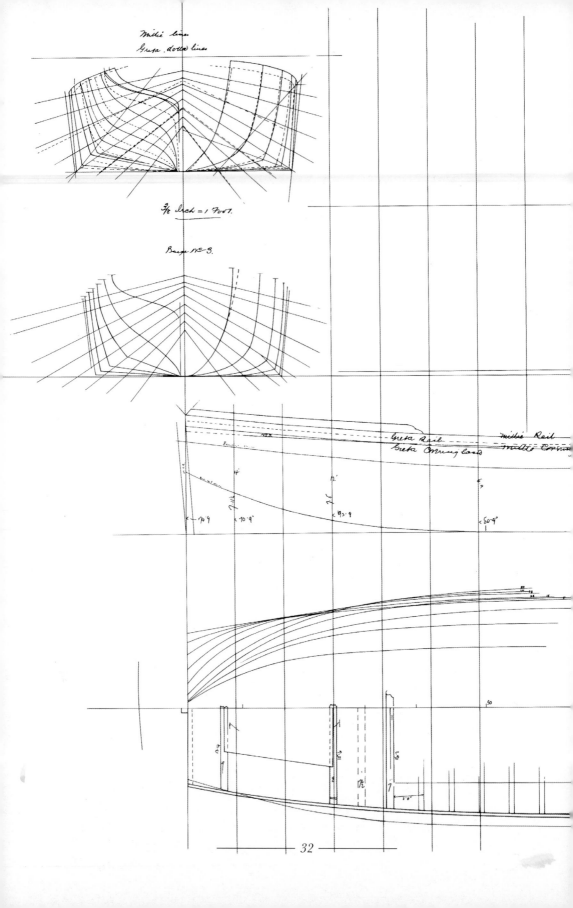

milli line
Greta dotted lines

3/8 Inch = 1 Foot.

Barge No 3.

Greta Rail ------ milli Rail
Greta Covering board ------ milli Covering

[Plans of the barges *Millie* and *Greta*]
The barges *Millie* and the *Greta* were built by Stone
Brothers at Brightlingsea from these plans. However
both of these wooden barges were actually slightly
different

The steel barge *Adieu* sailing in the Medusa Channel, which is a channel that links Harwich Harbour to the Wallet. Fred Horlock, a member of a large family of Mistley bargemen, had this barge built in 1929, at Mistley. He built up a considerable fleet of barges and small steamers, mostly to supply the mills at Mistley. The Horlocks were all very keen on barge racing and the barges that Fred had built at his shipyard down river of the quays were intended to achieve racing success. Between 1924-31 Horlock had seven steel barges, *Repertor*, *Portlight*, *Xylonite*, *Reminder*, *Adieu*, *Blue Mermaid* and the *Resourceful* built. The *Resourceful* was the last sailing barge built, but after only eighteen months she was converted to a motor barge. Fred Horlock's largest steamship was the 3,920 gross tons *Coralie Horlock*.

Right Top: The barge *Xylonite*, skippered by Richard Titchener, in Harwich Harbour. The *Xylonite* traded under sail until 1957. In 1985 the Cirdan Trust of Maldon bought her and she became the first of their fleet of youth training vessels. They laid her up in 2007 for a major refit.

When the Thames was the world's greatest commercial highway advertisements on barges' sails were very popular. It was one of the Mistley barges, *Volunteer*, which is reputed, in the late Victorian period, to have been the first barge to have advertisements on her sail. The barges that traded with Apollinaries mineral water to London had 'Apollinaries' painted on their sails. These were mostly boomies and were towed up the River Rhine. The carbonic rich mineral water was such a successful product that the music hall artist Vesta Tilley used to sing about 'Scotch and Polly.'

The *Cabby*, with Hays' logo in her tops'l, off Walton Naze with *Marjorie* in the background.

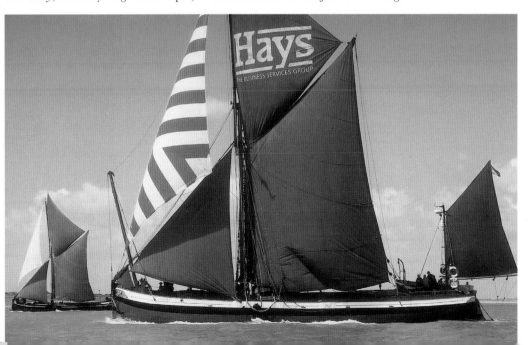

The *Lady Daphne* during the Pin Mill Sailing Barge Match.

Ray and Ben Payne's *Beric* in amongst the houseboats at Pin Mill. The *Beric* was built by J. & H. Cann in 1896 at Harwich for William Groom of Harwich, who named her after a cousin. Cann's barges were all well-built attractive craft, but *Beric* survived because she became one of the Ipswich mill barges. Because Cranfield Bros and R. & W. Paul's barges carried perishable cargoes, they had to be very well maintained. This work was done at the Dock End Shipyard, just outside the lock at Ipswich.

Aboard the barge *Thistle* in Ipswich Dock, 2005. On the left are Paul's and Cranfields' mills shortly before they were demolished. The backbone of the Ipswich barge trade had been supplying these mills.

The mulie barge *Ena* at Ipswich in 1998, shortly before she was sold. Paul's had owned the barge from the time she was built at Harwich in 1906 until they sold her about ninety-two years later.

Ipswich was the last port to have a fleet of barges working under sail. Paul's sold *Marjorie* and *Anglia* in 1960 and Cranfield's barges did cargoes from London under sail for a little longer, but mainly the barges were used for grain storage in the Dock. Cranfield's sold the *Venture* in 1963 and *May* the following year and after that *Spinaway C* did lightering and raced until 1967, when she was sold. The Ipswich motor barges continued to trade and in 1974 Paul's rigged out the *Ena* again for their social club. She was the last of the mill barges owned in the port.

The *Vigilant* passing Felixstowe Ferry on the way out of the River Deben bound for St Oysth, 2004. Orvis & Fuller built the *Vigilant* at Ipswich in 1904. When she was converted to a motor barge her main hatch coamings were raised to try and keep her cargo tonnage up and compensate for the space taken up by the engine.

Right: The *Thalatta* at the Ferry Quay, Woodbridge on one of her annual visits since 1975. The *Thalatta* was built at Harwich in 1906 and was originally rigged as a gaff ketch, a rig known to bargemen as a 'boomie.' When boomies went out of fashion, because they needed at least one extra hand, the gaff mains'l was replaced by a sprits'l, but the mizzen was retained. This rig was known as a 'mulie.' As a mulie R. & W. Paul of Ipswich put the *Thalatta* into the London-Ipswich grain trade.

The trade was bringing imported grain from the Royal Docks, London up to the mills at Ipswich. When road transport started to take away this trade the barges were finished. The Thames Barge Preservation Trust was formed to try and keep one barge trading under sail when all the others had to give up. The attractive Harwich-built barge *Memory* was purchased and between 1956-60 traded with the Horlock's of Mistley barges.

The Trust was then wound up and eventually the *Memory* was sold and used by the East Coast Sail Trust, backed by Hervey Benham, to run trips for school children from Maldon. In 1967 the East Coast Sail Trust sold the *Memory* and bought Paul's motor barge *Thalatta* and rigged her out again as a mulie barge, using the sailing gear and leeboards from the *Memory*.

Richard Johnson's barge yacht *Dinah* with the Tide Mill and its Granary at Woodbridge quay, 2006. The *Dinah* had come down from Southwold to Woodbridge on her first trip under sail for over thirty years.

The tripper boat *Lady Florence* at Orford Quay. Orford is one of the few complete barge ports to survive. On the left is Quay House, which was the home of the corn and coal merchant Edward Rope, who rented the quay and warehouses off the Sudbourne Hall Estate. Until 1939 coal was brought in from the North of England in the summer and stored in the brick warehouses ready for retailing in the winter.

The bargemen used to say that Snape was the most difficult port to reach on the East Coast. The narrow winding channel above Aldeburgh is marked with withies, small tree branches, but these are often knocked down and the channel can be difficult to follow. Here the *Cygnet* is leading the *Henry* up to the quay at the former Snape Maltings.

The *Cygnet*, skippered by Des Kaliszewski, returning to Snape Maltings.

The *Henry* arriving at Snape Quay, 2006. The *Henry* was built at Grays in 1904 for the local grain merchants Cole and Lecquire. She is rather smaller than most barges and finished trading in 1948, when she was sold to Arthur Bennett to become his sailing home.

The Maltings at Snape Bridge, at the top of the River Alde, were started in 1859 so that malt, made from locally-grown barley, could be transported to the Thames-side and Norwich breweries. The last commercial sailing barge up here was *Beatrice Maud* in 1939, but in 1965 motor barge traffic was started again and flourished for a few years taking building materials to the Cobra Mist Early Warning station on the Lantern Marshes, near Orfordness.

In 1954 I saw a barge come into the River Deben under sail. After work I cycled down to Ramsholt, sailed my dinghy down river and spoke to Arther Bennett on his barge *Henry*.

SAILING BARGES HULL LENGTHS, BEAM AND DEPTH

Adieu	87ft 9ins x 19ft 4ins x 6ft 4ins	*Marjorie*	84ft x 19ft 2ins x 6ft 2ins
Alice	77ft x 18ft x 4ft 2ins	*May*	81ft x 19ft x 6ft 6ins
Atrato	84ft 4ins x 18ft 6ins x 6ft 6ins	*Millie*	80ft 4ins x 19ft x 6ft 1ins
		Mirosa	82ft x 20ft 9ins x 5ins 6
Beatrice Maud	88ft 1in x 21ft 5ins x 7ft 1in		
Beric	83ft 6ins x 20ft 1in x 6ft 4ins	*Niagara*	86ft 7ins x 20ft 6ins x 6ft 7ins
		Nellie	79ft 3ins x 17ft 8ins x 5ft 2ins
Cabby	84ft x 21ft 3ins x 6ft 9ins		
Cambria	91ft 1in x 21ft 9ins x 7ft 3ins	*Orinoco*	86ft 6ins x 20ft 3ins x 6ft 2ins
Centaur	85ft 6ins x 19ft 5ins x 6ft 2ins		
Cygnet	41ft 8ins x 13ft 3ins x 3ft 8ins	*Phoenician*	84ft 1in x 20ft 8ins x 7ft 3ins
		Pudge	82ft 4ins x 21ft x 6ft 8ins
Dawn	82ft x 21ft 6in x 5ft 5ins		
Decima	85ft x 19ft 2ins x 6ft	*Reminder*	87ft 9ins x 19ft 4ins x 6ft 5ins
Dinah	45ft 3ins x 12ft 2ins x 5ft 1ins		
		Thalatta	88ft 9ins x 21ft 5ins x 7ft 1in
Edme	80ft x 17ft 9ins	*Thistle*	86ft x 19ft 5ins x 7ft 2ins
Ena	88ft 2ins x 19ft 5ins x 7ft 2ins		
		Victor	82ft 2ins x 20ft 3ins x 6ft
First Attempt	74ft 6ins x 14ft 10ins x 4ft 7ins	*Vigilant*	84ft x 20ft x 8ft 3ins
Gladys	84ft x 2ft 6ins	*Will ex Will Everard*	97ft 6ins x 23ft 1in x 9ft 6ins
Greta	80ft x 18ft 7ft x 5ft	*Wyvenhoe*	84ft x 18ft 6ins x 6ft 2ins
Henry	76ft 3ins x 18ft 1in x 5ft 1in	*Xylonite*	87ft x 18ft 6ins x 6ft
Hydrogen	94ft 8ins x 22ft x 7ft 3ins		
Ironsides	84ft x 20ft 3ins x 6ft 4ins		
Kathleen	82ft 9ins x 19ft 7ins		
Kitty	82ft x 20ft		
Lady Daphne	90ft 8ins x 21ft 4ins x 7ft 5ins		
Lady of the Lea	72ft x 13ft x 4ft 9ins		
Lord Alcester	101ft x 24ft x 8ft 8ins		
Lord Robert	82ft 8ins x 20ft x 5ft 8ins		

Chapter Two

BARGE AHOY! Barges paying their way.

12.5.5[?]

THE 68-TON BARGE XYLONITE, which competed in the Champion Bowsprit Class, racing alongside two other competitors early in the race.

SWAN SONG OF THAMES BARGES

LAST RACE BECOMES 15th VICTORY

DRIFT TO THE SEA

This morning's light westerly airs meant that the 46-mile race started with a drift from Gravesend down Seareach to the mouth. Leading from the start was F. T. Everard and Sons Ltd.'s 51-year-old Sara, which had 14 wins to her credit.

At the wheel was Mr. J. Uglow, 48, of Grange Road, Gravesend. Two other barges. Clara and Glenmore, had a woman in their crews.

At 12.25, when the Sara was off Southend Pier, the course was shortned by 20 miles. Six barges with only a few feet separating them followed her round the Royal Sovereign, the committee boat.

The wind increased steadily all the way up Seareach, with the barges heeling to the pull of their sails. On board here we could hear the music of sail as the barges passed.

Despite the fact that one of her crew fell overboard and she had to round up into the wind to pick him up, Sara maintained her lead. With every inch of her 5,800 feet of canvas pulling, she crossed the line first, winner for the 15th time.

Results : Champion Bowsprit Class: 1, Sara; 2, Xylonite; 3, Sirdar; 4, Nelson. Restricted Staysail Class : 1, Esther; 2, Revival; 3, Dreadnought; 4, Clara; 5, Westmoreland. Auxiliary Class : 1, Edith May; 2, Dawn; 3, Glenmore. Disqualified, Waterlily.

From Our SPECIAL CORRESPONDENT ABOARD M.V. ROYAL SOVEREIGN, Thursday.

The red-sailed Thames spritsail barges, the last "tall" ships to ply round Britain's coasts, had their swan song to-day when 13 of them raced in the Grand Coronation Barge Sailing Match. The race was organised by the Thames and Medway Barge Committees.

It was in 1863 that Mr. Henry Dodd, a barge skipper who made a fortune out of removing London's refuse, sponsored the first "match." Yesterday's was probably the last as it is generally agreed that "the barges are finished."

Used up and down the East and South coasts since the 17th century, there are now only 33 barges trading by sail alone. Even the 100 others with engines are not considered economical.

They cannot guarantee a regular arrival time. A new barge costs as much as £5,000; and a new set of sails £640, compared with £140 before the war.

The Coronation Thames Barge Race in 1953 was seen at the time as being 'the final swan song', in Sir Alan Herbert's words, of the spritsail barge. However it actually rekindled interest in racing barges. Everard's rigged out the *Sara*, *Veronica* and *Dreadnought* and their rivals, the London and Rochester Trading Co. rigged out the *Sirdar* just for the annual Thames and Medway races. These barges were given huge impractical sail plans which were expensive to maintain and in 1962 the companies decided to stop barge racing, on the centenary of Dodd's original Thames race. The Champion Class barges *Sara* and *Dreadnought* were broken up because the barge companies considered their usefulness to be at an end. In fact barge enthusiasts fought very hard to keep barges going and in 1962 the Blackwater and Pin Mill Barge Matches were started for privately-owned barges not involved in cargo-carrying.

The Champion Class barges had pushed flat-bottomed barges to their sailing limit; the *Sirdar* had been timed at 13 knots in one Thames race, but she had Dutch leeboards, and a far larger sail area in cotton, not flax, than a crew of two could have managed when trading. The true function of a barge was to have a two-man sailing cargo carrier, but this was lost in the battle to win prizes.

During the brief period before 1962 bargemen enjoyed being paid to sail the Champion Barges, but didn't take them very seriously. They did, however, approve of Everard's introducing the practice for putting leeboard winches on blocks, because it made working them slightly less back-breaking. The pre-war barges had carried large headsails for racing, but huge yachty 'candy striped' headsails were regarded with horror, by most barge-men at the time. When the *Sara* and *Veronica* and *Dreadnought* finished sailing, spars and leeboards were sold and used by other barges.

In the cutting a large headsail is being hauled out on the *Xylonite's* bowsprit. That sail was still aboard when I sailed aboard her as mate three years later. Although very useful in light weather, it was very hard work for one man to haul it out from the fo'c'sle and set it.

The St Osyth charter bowsprit barge *Edme* sailing at 8 knots in the Pin Mill Sailing Barge Match, 2006. This barge loaded 110 and a quarter tons and was built by Cann at Harwich in 1898. When light she draws about 2ft 10ins of water, but with her leeboards fully lowered she draws 18ft. At the time the *Edme* and the *Mirosa* were the only barges without engines. They were also two of the most consistent prizewinners in the five main races because they didn't drag a propeller.

In the trading era, a barge fitted with an engine was referred to in official records as being an 'auxiliary barge,' but bargemen would have none of this. Once an engine was fitted they were referred to as being a 'motor barge' as distinct from the original 'sailormen.' A barge with an engine is a totally different craft from a pure sailing barge, although in practical terms an engine allowed a barge to earn more carrying cargoes and, more recently, be much more competitive in charter work. On a calm day a barge under sail moves silently through the water like a bird through the air.

The *Edme*, with a charter party aboard, with skipper Andy Harman at the wheel. She traded under sail until 1949 before she became one of Brown's lighters taking timber up to their Heybridge yard, from ships anchored off Osea Island. When she was rigged out again for sailing in 1992 a Seager-made 'chaff cutter' steering wheel off the *Mistley* was acquired from one of the barge hulks on Northey Island. To get the barge sailing leeboard winches, made by Gardiners of Sittingbourne, were bought.

Powered leeboard winches were fitted on the *May* in 2007 because the crew found hand winches difficult with 40 passengers aboard. The *Edme*, which has been kept as a traditional sailing barge, was withdrawn from racing as a protest to draw the line and prevent traditional working craft from being turned into yachts.

The windlass on the *Edme*.

Northdown and *Wyvenhoe*, 1984

Hoisting the *Edme's* mast using the windlass. Being able to lower the masts made the spritty barges more versatile, because it allowed them to go under bridges. Barges could sail up to a bridge, have the mast lowered, go under with the tide and have it hoisted again. Usually when they did this a 'huffler,' an unofficial pilot who helped work the barge, was hired to help get the mast up.

The *Edme* waiting for enough water to berth alongside Prior's Fingringhoe wharf in 2002. Coming up the River Colne is Prior's *Bert Prior* returning from the London River for another freight of ballast. The Prior 'ballastmen' took ballast from the Quarry at Fingringhoe to the London wharves for the building trade and at that time were the only cargo vessels operating regularly for an Essex owner.

Only a few sailing barges have survived, remember in the Edwardian era there were over two thousand of them; but the trade they were built to serve has totally vanished. Quays and warehouses of the barge coast now stand empty or are given over to yachts or housing. Time never stands still.

Skipper Andy Harman watches as Prior's loads the *Edme* with 52 tons of sand, 2002. The skipper has to make sure that the barge being loaded is floating evenly.

Right Top: Reuben Chappell's ship's portrait of the boomie barge *Harold*, built by White at Sittingbourne in 1900 and loaded 180 tons. The flat-bottomed, flat-sided barge with leeboards was such a success in the Thames Estuary that owners looked for some form of barge to go into the general coastal trade. The result was the 'boomie,' a barge with a gaff ketch rig, often with counter stern and clipper bow. Fine craft, but the gaff main-sail required at least another man to handle it so they were more expensive to operate than a spritty, but better in the English Channel seas.

Apart from the extra hands needed on the boomies, another disadvantage was that when sailing in the rivers they were not as handy as the spritties. When the the Horlocks at Mistley bought the *Harold* they put 'wangs' to the end of the mains'l gaff to try and make her sail closer to the wind.

'Sprittie' barges remained smaller than the boomie barges until wire rigging was introduced. Then larger sprit-ties were built because the wire 'wangs' allowed them to control the sprit mains'l at sea. The *Harold* was still a boomie when she was lost on the Lincolnshire coast in 1928.

Right Bottom: The *Centaur* sailing in Ipswich Dock to berth with the *Ena*, 1987. She has the five sail 'staysail' or 'stem head' rig. In the trading era most of the Essex and Suffolk barges had bowsprits, jibs and jib tops'ls, because they made long passages down the Swin and Wallet, but in the revival era many barges just have a stay-sail rig to keep down expenses.

The stays'l barge *Wyvenhoe* in the Pin Mill Barge Match, 2004. During 1898, Forrest & Sons at Wivenhoe built the steel barges *Atrato*, *Niagara* and *Wyvenhoe*. The *Wyvenhoe* was built for a Greenwich wharf owner who wanted her to win races. The London and Rochester Trading Co. converted her to a motor barge with a wheelhouse and single cargo hatch. In 1982 Richard Walsh bought her out of trade and converted her back to a sailing barge with two hatches and used some of the gear from his wooden barge, the *Kathleen*.

The *Pudge* sailing on the River Blackwater in a strong breeze. To reduce the sail area, on a barge, the mains'l is 'picked up' in the brails in a strong wind, which effectively reefs the sail. The tops'l is sometimes 'rucked' by dropping it down, but leaving it sheeted out to the end of the sprit.

A 'stackie,' with her topmast 'housed' (down) waits for the flood tide to go up under Tower Bridge in about 1910.

A stackie barge leaving Brightlingsea in about 1910. The mate and huffler standing on the top of the stack had to shout directions down to the skipper at the wheel.

The *Cygnet* in 2003. Des Kaliszewski had loaded the hold with blocks and then a 'stack' on the deck and spent the winter sailing single handed on the East Coast.

In the early nineteenth century small barges were carrying hay up the Thames to feed the London street horses. This trade grew, so that by the end of the Victorian era 'muck and straw' barges, or 'stackies', were being loaded in many creeks in Essex, Suffolk and Kent. The stack freights were not always to London. The most unusual freights were hay from Boyton Dock on the Butley River for the pit ponies in the North, but I doubt if these were deck cargoes.

Sometime mangolds were loaded in the hold and used to feed the London cows in their milking barns. Trusses of hay or straw were loaded half-way up the mast, which on a full-sized barge was about 10-12ft above the deck. The straw and hay were notoriously slippery and to hold the deck cargo in place 'stack irons,' three or four on either side rail, were put in place to try and prevent the stack from moving. Many barges retained their stack irons and used them when loading deck cargoes of timber.

On the stackie barges a spar was placed across the after end of the stack to prevent the mainsheet from chafing on the stack. The mains'l and fores'l had reef points so they could be lifted above the stack and the mains'l had a very high-cut peak so that the sail would continue to drive the barge along. Bob Wells, who sailed on Wrinch's *Snowdrop* with his father in the 1930s, said that the draught had funnelled around behind the straw and they believed it helped to push the barge along.

In the Thames the stackie skippers liked to get under way on the first of the flood tide in order to reach Tower Bridge before 'tide time,' high water, when the river was very busy with tugs and lighters coming out of the Docks. The masts on the stackies were lowered to go above Tower Bridge and they were then rowed and towed on the tide up to various wharves.

'London violets' was the term the bargemen called their return cargoes of muck. Wrinch of Holbrook had the last barges in the straw and muck trade until 1939. A lady who grew up in Holbrook in the 1930s recalled, 'You always knew when the men who worked on those barges were coming, phew!'

Gerard Swift pointing to the bungs in the bottom of the stackie barge *Dawn*. These were used to let water into the hold to scrub out the barge after the return freight of the horse muck.

The *Dawn* was built in 1897 for the Maldon hay and straw merchant James Keeble. Keeble hired a former shipyard at Maldon and asked the young shipwrights, Walter Cook and his brother-in-law Woodward, to build a barge for the stackie trade. Cook had worked for the renowned Maldon builder Howard and followed his practice of a composite, wooden hull with iron deck beams. When she was launched the river wall was dug away to slip her into the water, but she got stuck and was not launched until the following day.

Because straw was a very light freight, the *Dawn* does not have very high sides, but is beamy compared to other barges, to give stability. She is reputed to have been the only Maldon barge not to lose a stack freight overboard between the Blackwater and the Thames.

When petrol engines replaced horses the little groups of 'hay-stacks' that sailed up the Thames on the tide vanished. With the *Dawn* the ammonia from muck had caused major rot in the hull and the barge had to have a major rebuild in 1928. To get a new keelson in, Cooks sank the barge and floated it into place through the bow. The barge then traded mostly with timber and grain until the early 1960s, but by that time an engine had been fitted.

Most wooden barges had bungs and when they were old and sold off as houseboats in creeks their owners saved time pumping by pulling out the bung at low tide. Sometimes owners forgot to replace the bungs as the tide rose. Once the Duke family, who lived on *Leslie West* at Pin Mill, suddenly found their home filling with water. This happened twice to the White family aboard the stumpie barge *First Attempt*, in Oare Creek.

The original 1891 aft skipper's cabin on the barge *May*. This was more or less a standard layout, although instead of two drawers behind the table there was normally a cupboard known as the 'Yarmouth Roads' because, like the anchorage, it was large and damp.

The aft cabin of the *Cambria* in 1967. This was typical of a barge skipper's quarters, although larger because she was a coasting barge. The skipper's bunk was by tradition on the starboard side and the mate's on the port, both with sliding doors so that the crew could sleep during the day.

The *Marjorie*, built by R. & W. Paul at Ipswich in 1902. Her bowsprit has been 'picked up,' a practice that work-ing barges always did when they went into rivers and docks. The jib is ballooned out, as she is racing and has a large crew.

Most barges were about the same length on deck, but the beam and depth of the hull made a tremendous difference to the amount of cargo they could load. The *Marjorie* was a slightly larger barge than the *May*, but they both loaded 125 tons of grain because *Marjorie's* cabin took up more space. The barge *Reminder* was again roughly the same size but loaded 140 tons because she had a steel hull and the sides of the barge acted as the side of the hold. The wooden barges were 'lined' with two and a half-inch planks which took a lot of space out of the hold, so that they loaded less cargo in the same sized hold. The steel barges just had an iron frame down the centre of the hold, while the wooden barges had a high 'keelson,' internal keel, running the full length of the barge.

Right Top: The steel mulie barge *Thistle* sailing in the Wallet. A powerful barge, claimed to have sailed at 13 knots in the Swin on passage to the Thames. This barge was built of steel at Port Glasgow in 1895 and was the only Thames barge built in Scotland. *Thistle* loaded 150 tons to sea and 170 tons in the rivers.

Right: The windlass on the *Gladys* is driven by a motor to save hard work on the handles. This was a replacement from her former coasting barge windlass that had a post in the middle. Also on the windlass is the winch for the 'dolly line' for wrapping around in docks.

The *Gladys*, built by J. & H. Cann at Harwich in 1901, loaded about 160 tons of grain. In 1950 her owners, Cranfield Bros of Ipswich, had her fitted with an engine that took up space at the aft end of the hold and to overcome this her hatch coamings (sides) were heightened, so that she could continue to load a full cargo.

With cargoes such as barley, maize and oats, which 'weighed light', the mill barges could increase the size of the hold by putting the hatches along the top of the coamings on their sides. This effectively created a larger hold, but the normal hatch clothes wouldn't cover these enlarged hatch sides. However sheets were hired from the railway companies to keep the cargoes dry. Flour was another 'light freight' and sacks were stacked above the hatch coamings, again large sheets were put over the top and roped down very tightly, because they had to arrive dry. In modern times with green hatch clothes, but before World War I they were black with tar.

George Gooderham's Snape-based *Redoubtable* when Headly Farrington was skipper in 1973.

The *Redoubtable* had a very beamy hull for carrying bulky cargoes to the mills at Mistley. She loaded 180 tons from London-Great Yarmouth and once delivered 200 tons from London to Mistley and loaded 220 tons when doing river lightering, all with a crew of two. After being sold she was taken on a publicity voyage from Lerwick to Peterhead but was blown across to Norway. She was broken up later.

Skipper Dave Copsey at the wheel of Tops'l Charter's barge *Thistle*. Only the coasting barges had wheel shelters, but all barges had a brake on the wheel so that the skipper could lock it and go on deck and help handle the gear.

The *Ironsides* was built at West Thurrock in 1900. Because she was built of steel and had a deep hull the *Ironsides* probably loaded about 30 tons more than a wooden barge of the same length.

Ironsides was 'cut down' to a motor barge in 1939, but in 1968 Alan Reekie bought her and she was rigged out and became a very successful racing barge, particularly after he introduced the hollow steel leeboards. In 1987 Mark Tower bought *Ironsides* and developed the booking agency 'Topsail Charters and Events' around her.

The steel barge *Reminder* on a charter trip in the River Orwell. In the trading days a barge's earning power was ruled by the amount of cargo it could load, but in the charter era the number of passengers carried is the deciding factor.

Stephanie Valentine and Paul Jefferies started Tops'l Charters of Maldon in 1987 with the idea of preserving barges by keeping them sailing. In 2006 Tops'l Charters of Maldon organized charter work, mostly day trips, for five sailing barges. Tops'l Charters owns the *Hydrogen* that has a MCA licence to carry 50 people, the *Thistle* takes 50 people and the *Reminder* 12. They also take bookings for the *Cabby*, which takes 40 people and is based at Maldon and the *Repertor* that takes 12 people and is based at Faversham.

The *Cabby* returning to the Hythe, Maldon with a charter party aboard. The *Cabby* has a sunken cockpit in the aft end of the main hold. The cockpit in the hold was an idea first designed for *Sirdar* by William Collard.

When there were no cargoes for the sailing barges, owners sort other ways to make them pay and passenger trips and racing have kept the barges sailing. In 1961, 'charter' barges, carrying passengers, started at Maldon with the *Marjorie*, skippered by Fred Cooper. The following summer Peter Light, who had been a skipper in trading barges, became skipper of the *Marjorie*. He won the first revived Maldon Barge Match in 1962. The *Marjorie* had cabins in the hold, but when *Memory* started running trips from Mill Beach in 1962 there was no money for cabins so that 'charterers' slept in hammocks, a practice the *Thalatta* continues.

John Fairbrother had been skipper of Cranfield Bros sailing barges at Ipswich and later rigged out the *Kitty* for chartering from Maldon. John sailed the *Kitty* without an engine, until the council put yacht moorings in the channel and he could no longer 'turn' (the bargemen's term of tacking) up to the Hythe.

Because the channel is narrow at Maldon the *Hydrogen's* bow has been run on to the mud so that the flood tide will push the stern around and she can berth at the Hythe with her bow pointing down river, ready to leave. Another method of turning in a narrow channel was to let the anchor go and swing around.

The wooden mulie barge *Hydrogen* was built at Rochester by Gill in 1906 as a tanker to load 200 tons of cre-osote to trade to Grangemouth on the Firth of Forth. The *Hydrogen's* skipper, Arthur Coward, a hard sailor, carried a gilded cockerel at the masthead and this annoyed the other skippers who told him to 'take that thing down.' Coward said he would when anyone could beat his record in 1921 of 24 hours from Spurn Head to Milton Creek, but no-one did!

The *Will* was built at Great Yarmouth for Everard's of Greenhithe as the *Will Everard* of London in 1925 and was one of four big steel mulie barges built for the coasting trade. Originally she loaded 295 tons, but after an engine had been fitted only 240 tons of grain could be loaded. Although considerably larger than most coasting barges, it was her deep hull that gave her a high loading capability. In the Victorian period several large barges were built of wood and given schooner, brigantine and even barque rigs, but their flat bottoms and large leeboards were a trouble in the open sea. Much smaller river barges didn't have a long enough waterline to make them effective sailers, but barges with a length of around 80-90ft on deck were the most efficient.

Mark Tower at the wheel of his steel barge *Will* of Maldon. The *Will* is in the charter trade from St Katharine's Docks, London, and can carry 59 passengers. Her present sail plan is much smaller than she had in the coasting trade, but she has around 150 tons of ballast, equivalent to being half loaded, giving her a draft of around 7ft.

The coaster's windlass on the *Will* with the central pawl.

Will Everard loading wheat at the Customs House Creek, King's Lynn, in 1955. After loading wheat, we had an uneventful passage to Hull.

Chapter Three

NEW HULLS FROM OLD The shipwrights art.

The barge *Memory* abandoned on the saltings at Tollesbury. Built by Cann in 1904 the *Memory* had been regarded as one of the handiest barges to sail and was bought in 1956 by the Sailing Barge Preservation Society who intended to keep her trading under sail, but ten years later she was an unrigged hull lying in Saltcote Creek.
  In Heybridge Creek are the white bones of the *Beaumont Belle*, built by John Howard at the Shipways yard, Maldon in 1894. She was dumped after being one of Sadd's lighters that brought timber up the Blackwater from ships anchored off Osea Island. The *Beaumont Belle* was built for the farmer Alan Stanford of Beaumont Hall at the head of Walton Backwaters.

Howard was renowned for building very attractive barges, mostly for farm work. He believed his most attractive barge was the 82ft x 19ft x 5ft 10ins *Saltcote Belle* that was built in 1895 and named after a cow which had given seven gallons of milk in a day.

Which barges have survived is purely a matter of luck; it depends if the owner wants to keep the barge sailing and has the financial resources to keep up the endless replacement work. In 1964 I sailed on *Memory* in the Pin Mill Race and she was really no different to most of the other barges taking part. I have also sailed on the *Sirdar, Millie, Lord Roberts, Redoubtable, Convoy* and *Spinaway C* which might have been sailing today, if there had been the resources to keep up the endless maintenance and renewals.

The mulie barge *Cambria* at Eastern Counties Farmers' quay, Ipswich Wet Dock in 1970. Skipper Bob Roberts and his mate had hauled the *Cambria* from the dock gate up to ECF with a dolly line. This freight of cattle cake from Tilbury was the last commercial cargo delivered by a sail-only barge in northern Europe. She loaded 170 tons to sea on a depth of 7ft.6ins but only drew 3ft when light.

The Greenhithe barge builder F.T. Everard thought his sons should each build a barge, so William built the *Cambria* and his brother Fred the barge *Hibernia* in 1906. The *Hibernia* was lost on the Norfolk coast in 1937, by which time Will and Fred Everard were building up the largest coastal fleet, under the British flag. In the 1950s F.T. Everard & Sons had over one hundred motor ships, but they kept the *Will Everard*, which had an engine, and the *Cambria*. In 1964 the *Cambria* was sold to her skipper Bob Roberts, an outspoken bargeman, folk singer and author, and he continued to trade her under sail until 1970. She was the last British registered vessel to carry commercial cargoes under sail. After that the *Cambria* became part of the Maritime Trust fleet; they kept her tied up to quays and opened her to the public, but this never raised enough money to maintain her properly. In 1996 the rotten hull, one of the finest wooden spritty barges ever built, was given to the Cambria Trust.

Members of the Cambria Trust on the coasting barge *Cambria* at Camber, Sheerness celebrating the fact that the Heritage Lottery Fund had given them a grant to totally rebuild the barge, 2007. If the Cambria Trust had not received a grant to cover most of the rebuild the barge may well have been dumped, with the other barge hulks, in Shepherds Creek behind the nearby Deadman's Island.

The *Cambria* was built with the luxury of a wheel shelter with a tiny toilet, a bucket and seat, in the whaleback of the shelter, at a time when most barges had an open wheel and 'bucket and chuck it' toilet. To the end of working sail most barges had just a dip bucket on a rope for a crew's toilet. The *Will Everard*, built in 1925, had a toilet, which emptied overboard, in the back of the wheel shelter, but to flush it the crew had to draw up a bucket of water.

The starboard pump head and leeboard winch, by T. Seager of Faversham, on the *Cambria*. Barges had hand pumps at each corner of their hold as the wooden barges 'made water' most of the time.

The leeboard winch is on chocks, which made less back-breaking work for the crew, a development from Everard's champion racing barges, which has become standard. A rope brake on the winch controls the leeboards so that they do not 'take charge' and bang down too quickly. The drum on the side of the winch is for hauling in the 'wang' (vang) to the end of the main sprit to make the barge sail closer to the wind. A great advantage when sailing in the Thames and other confined waters.

The great secret of the spritsail barge was the use of winches that allowed two men to handle the barge's vast area of sail, but even then it was very hard work.

Dave Speight working on his new steel barge *British King* at Walton on the Naze 1999. Dave Speight bought the wooden *British King*, a stackie barge built by Cook at Maldon in 1901, and rigged her out for charter work, but in the end the hull had to be broken up. The new *British King*, built on the lines of Goldsmith's steel barges, has never been launched, but in 2006 the hull was taken by road in four sections to Redcar for use in making a film about the Dunkirk Evacuation.

Jonathon & Richard Webb rebuilt the steel *Melissa*, at Pin Mill in 2005. When craft are rebuilt they are nearly always altered slightly, *Melissa's* sides were increased by 7 inches to give more headroom for passengers in the hold.

Richard Johnson's *Dinah*, skippered by Hys Olink, on one of her first sails for over thirty years, in the River Deben, 2006.

Gerry Brown finishing off the rebuilding of the barge-yacht *Dinah* at Southwold in 2004. The *Dinah* was built by Gill & Sons of Rochester, in 1887, but by the 1970s her hull had worn out. She was rebuilt over the decades in various places and work was completed at Southwold.

Tim Goldsack and his shipwrights Geoff 'Frog' Ingle, Jon Hall and Robin Miller were the main team involved with rebuilding the barge *Dawn* at Heybridge Basin. The rebuild took two and a half years and only part of the bottom of the original hull remained. The new 2007 hull was built considerably stronger than the 1897 hull. The new keelson was laminated and English oak was used for the floors and frames. All the straight work and decking was done with the West African hardwood opepe while the planking is iroko, and the lining for the hold and 'ceiling' douglas fir.

Richard Daniels of BBC Television on the *Dawn* with buckets for mixing tar and horse muck. Barges with wooden hulls had two layers of planks with 'tar and set work' in between to keep them watertight. The tar and set work was a mixture of cow hair, cow muck and tar, which didn't go hard and allowed the hull to move and stay watertight. For *Dawn's* rebuild, roofing felt, with a mixture of tar and sticky horse muck, was used.

The Management team which rebuilt the sailing barge *Dawn*. Left to right: Russell Clarke, Maldon District Council, Robert Simper, Chairman Dawn Sailing Barge Trust; Colin South, Project Manager and Tom Wright, Heritage Lottery Fund Monitor.

In the 1970s Britain attempted to save its historic craft with a partly Government-funded Maritime Trust, but this proved to be too expensive. The *Dawn* was the first barge to be funded by the Heritage Lottery Fund when its policy had become to back local projects. Certainly the *Dawn's* rebuild was greatly aided by guidance from the Lottery monitor Tom Wright.

The smack *Varuna* and other Colchester smacks laid up at Johnny Milgate's yard, Peldon in 2006. The last smacks worked with just a derrick and tables on deck for sorting out oysters. The *Iris Mary* was oyster-dredging under power at Tollesbury until March 1985, at West Mersea. *Our Boys* and the 35ft *Puritan* went on a little longer and Southerly Frost's *Varuna* at Tollesbury was the last to be worked. In 2007 she was taken to David Patient's yard at Fullbridge, Maldon to be rebuilt.

The Milgate yard was built as the 'Shell Factory' and between 1920-24 smacks sailed up here with old oyster shells that were ground up for chicken grit. Just before World War II the Shell Factory machinery was sold to Germany as scrap but Johnny Milgate wonders if it might have come back in the form of bombs!

Our Boys, built at Paglesham in 1911, in a poor state on a hard at Rowhedge in 1999. The *Our Boys* appears to have still been dredging oysters under sail from West Mersea until just after World War II.

The totally rebuilt smack *Our Boys* sailing off Colne Point.

Dick Norris on his 40ft x 13ft x draft 5ft 6ins Whitstable 'yawl'(smack) *Stormy Petrel* at Gillingham after a rebuild in 2002. Dick bought the *Stormy Petrel* in 1962 and always sailed her without an engine. In the rebuild he kept as near as possible to her original state as a Whitstable work boat. With this authentic rebuild Dick Norris 'set the standard,' just as Mike Frost had done with the *Boadicea* about thirty years before.

Launching the Colne smack *Maria* 47ft 9ins x 10ft 8ins x draft 6ft at St Osyth in 2007. The *Maria* (pronounced *Mariah*) was built in 1866 by Harris Bros at Donyland (renamed Rowhedge in 1912.). Harris was mainly a yacht builder and the *Maria* is narrower than the later smacks which had more beam for stability in heavy weather. In 1996 Paul Winter tracked the *Maria* down to The Netherlands and had her brought back to Kent by lorry. At Andy Harman's yard at St Osyth the shipwrights rebuilt the *Maria*.

The Frinton and Walton Heritage Trust's 43ft pulling and sailing lifeboat *James Stevens No 14* being rebuilt, with a grant from the Heritage Lottery Fund, at Walton in 2005. Built at the Thames Ironworks in 1900 the *James Stevens* was fitted with an engine in 1906 and is claimed to be the first motor lifeboat. She was orginally based on the beach at Walton on the Naze, but until just after World War II lay out on a mooring just south of the pier.

John Cragie with the sailing RNLI lifeboat *Alfred Corry* at Southwold. The *Alfred Corry* was built in 1893 to the design of John's great-grandfather, another John Cragie who was also her first coxswain.

Because there is mostly shallow water on the East Coast the local craft had to be shoal draft, but have a way of gripping the water to sail against the wind. The barges had leeboards, the cockle boats centreboards, the longshore fishing boats at Southwold a plank as a leeboard, but the *Alfred Corry* had about 4 tons in water aboard, in tanks, to put her down so that she could go to windward. Before returning to the landing near Southwold harbour the water had to be pumped out of the tanks by hand.

Chapter Four

THE SMACKS Fishing under sail.

The 30ft x 12ft 11ins transom-sterned smack *Boadicea* was built in 1808 for dredging oysters in the Blackwater estuary off Mersea Island. The *Boadicea* (pronounced the old way) is dredging on the Common Ground; the Tollesbury & Mersea Oyster Co grounds are just up the river. When *Boadicea* was rebuilt in the 1880s her original clinker planking was replaced with carvel planking. The smack was totally rebuilt again in about 1972 by Mike Frost and is still sailed by his grandson, Ruben Frost.

The eighteenth century Essex smacks had clinker hulls with a 'pink' (pointed stern) and then transom sterns, but in the mid-nineteenth century, short counter sterns, known as 'tuck' sterns, were introduced.

Strictly speaking the Blackwater is the fresh water river, but the name is now used for the tidal estuary. The old name for the tidal estuary was The Pont and in the 1950s fishermen still said 'We came up Pont' meaning 'We came up the River.'

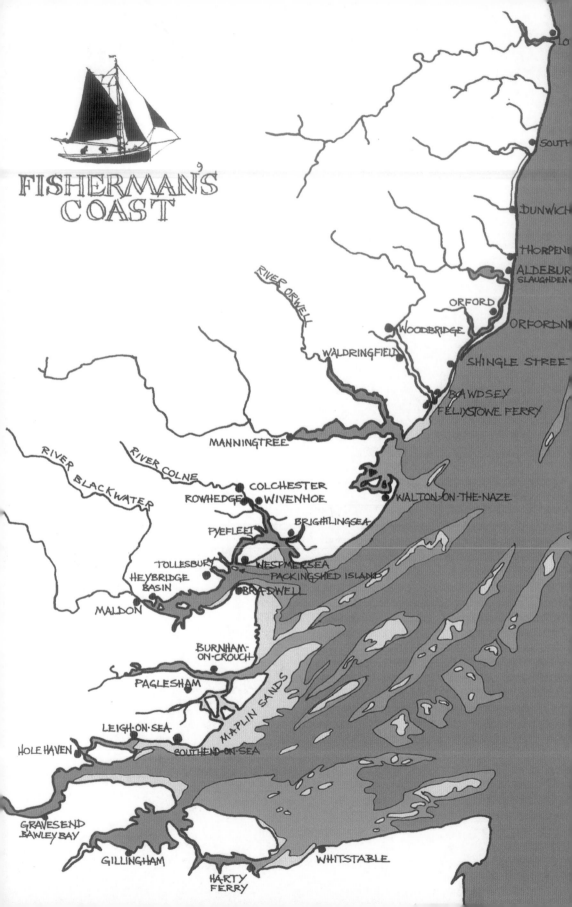

FISHERMAN'S COAST

LO

SOUTH

DUNWICH

THORPEN

ALDEBUR
SLAUGHDEN

ORFORD

RIVER ORWELL

WOODBRIDGE

ORFORDN

WALDRINGFIELD

SHINGLE STREET

BAWDSEY

FELIXSTOWE FERRY

MANNINGTREE

RIVER COLNE

RIVER BLACKWATER

COLCHESTER

ROWHEDGE   WIVENHOE

WALTON-ON-THE-NAZE

PYEFLEET

BRIGHTLINGSEA

TOLLESBURY   WESTMERSEA

HEYBRIDGE
BASIN

PACKINGSHED ISLAND

BRADWELL

MALDON

BURNHAM-
ON-CROUCH

PAGLESHAM

MAPLIN SANDS

LEIGH-ON-SEA

HOLE HAVEN

SOUTHEND-ON-SEA

GRAVESEND
BAWLEY BAY

GILLINGHAM

WHITSTABLE

HARTY
FERRY

The lute-sterned smack *Mary*, on her mooring at West Mersea. This smack, rebuilt by Brian Kennell, was probably built originally at Burnham-on-Crouch in the 1860s. The lute stern, a transom with an extended deck built out over it, was known in Essex as a 'whistle stern'. It appears to be halfway between a transom and counter stern.

Another mid-nineteenth century feature retained on the West Mersea smack *Mary* is the forestay made up to the stem head with a deadeye and lanyard.

The 46ft 5ins lute-sterned smack *William & Emily* on the new Brightlingsea Hard outside the former 'Anchor' pub. The *William & Emily* is reputed to have been built in the Channel Islands in the 1830s, but she was rebuilt by Drakes at Tollesbury at 'odd times' and became known as the *Odd Times*. She was totally rebuilt again by Dave Quested in 2004. The connection with the Channel Islands was that in the mid-Victorian period the larger Essex smacks sailed to Gorey, Jersey to dredge oysters near the French coast.

  The smacks of about 40ft went trawling in the Thames Estuary during the summer and 'stowboating' for sprat in the winter.   Many of the smackmen sailed as professional crews on the great yachts in the summer. Smack builders on the River Colne also built yachts, so the smacks were built with counter sterns and straight stems, similar to the Victorian yachts. However, they still retained the robust all-weather characteristics of workboats. The skippers who raced the big yachts often had a smack built with the prize money and the Colnesiders were so used to racing that they had to have fast smacks.

The lute stern of the *William & Emily*.

A stow net about to be lowered from the bows of the smack *G & A* while at anchor in the Blackwater Estuary, 2005. Because the channels in the Thames Estuary are narrow it was very difficult to undertake drift net fishing for sprat, therefore 'stow nets' were used. These were developed from medieval 'stall' nets where the craft anchored and a long bag of net was lowered down into the water over the smack's bow between two beams.

The bottom 'baulk' (beam) is about to slip down the 'wind chain' to open the mouth of the net. Malcolm MacGregor, who had gone 'stowboating' on the 43ft *Charlotte Ellen* in about 1951, made this stow net the previous winter, from an old trawl, with 17ft baulks for easy handling. Traditionally the whole net was much larger with 'baulks' of around 27ft long and a 42ft deep net mouth.

The 42ft smack *George & Alice* was built at Brightlingsea in 1909 for George and Alice Stokes of West Mersea. When their son went off to fight in World War I the smack was laid-up. He was reported 'missing in action,' but as the Stokes refused to believe that he was not coming back the smack remained waiting in a creek for years.

Paul Winter, Lucy Harris, Jonathan Simper and Malcolm MacGregor hauling the stow net on the *G & A*. This catch was mostly herring, many of which were put back into the river. In about 1922 the first engines, 15hp Kelvins, were put into Tollesbury smacks and Brightlingsea, Wivenhoe and Rowhedge smacks also had engines fitted soon afterwards. After World War II powerful engines became available and Whitstable and Leigh boats began to use Danish Larsen trawls for sprat, only the older smacks with low- powered engines went on stow netting until the early 1950s. After that Young's of Leigh used a small stow net for whitebait until 1964.

Cabin stove chimney on the *G & A*. The voyage home was time for a smack's crew to relax and hope there was a market for the fish they had caught.

On the right is Steve Richardson's smokehouse beside his shop at Orford. In the smokehouse the fish are hung over the slow burning oak wood fire to be 'cold smoked', not cooked, and this preserves the fish. With William Pinney's shop next door, selling fish smoked in the Gedgrave smokehouse, Orford has become a centre for smoked food sales. Before 1939 many fishing villages had smokehouses.

At Brightlingsea on a still day in November, at the height of the season, the smell of sprat being smoked prevailed across the whole town. Most of the smokehouses were small backyard 'sentry boxes' operated by the crews, while the main catch was pickled in barrels for export. During 1910, Mr Stewart of Newhaven, Scotland had introduced pickling in salt for export to the Baltic and Netherlands. Soon after this the Liverpool merchants Musson opened a pickling yard in Tower Street, Brightlingsea, and George Tabor Ltd also had a yard. The principal picklers became the Anglo-Swedish Preservation Union, who started a pickling yard on the waterfront in 1914. Most the yards used bay leaves to give flavour, but the Anglo-Swedish's secret was that they used sandalwood, that gave off a sweet smell. All these yards closed when World War II commenced.

James Edgar & Sons of Deal opened a cannery at Brightlingsea and fishermen landed their catches into the schooner *Gloria* that lay in the Pyefleet. However this firm went out of business and in 1932 Lewis Worp opened the North Sea Canners at Wivenhoe which eventually closed in about 1960.

Gwen Buckenham with Norwegian herring, which had been in salt over night, on a 'balk' ready to be 'cold smoked' into kippers at the Old Smoke House in Ragland Street, Lowestoft, 2000.

Left: The smack *Pioneer*, tacking down the River Orwell with a charter party aboard. She is the only surviving 'skillinger', a name given to the smacks that went dredging in the North Sea off the Dutch island of Terchelling. Even in the eighteenth century there were more smacks based on the River Colne than the local waters could support so they had to go farther afield. The larger Essex smacks used to work oyster grounds all around the coast of Britain and as they frequently raided oyster beds, between the Friesian Islands and Solway Firth, were regarded in many places to be oyster pirates.
  At Ramsholt on the River Deben an oyster fishery was established twice, in 1750 and again in 1884, and each time the Essexmen turned up and dredged up the whole lot, leaving just a few old shells. They also raided the beds at Orford, but in the late 1940s Richard Pinney re-established Macfisheries oyster layings in the Butley River. To find a market for his oysters, and the output from his smokehouse, Pinney opened the renowned Butley Orford Oysterage restaurant on Bakers Lane, Orford.

The 69ft 1in x 15ft 2ins draft 7ft *Pioneer* on the Hard at Brightlingsea in 2003, waiting to be floated after being totally rebuilt by Brian Kennell and Shaun White. The *Pioneer* was built in 1864 at Donyland (Rowhedge) as a cutter smack, but after the loss of several Brightlingsea cutter smacks while deepwater oyster dredging, she was cut in half and lengthened by 11ft in 1889. In the 1920s Tom Poole, foreman of the Colchester Oyster Fishery, bought up the old scalloping smacks *Pioneer*, *Hilda*, *Vanduara* and *Guide* and tried to revive the fishery. However, the crews were reluctant to go to sea in this hard trade and the last voyage was probably made in about 1931.

Steve Hall with an oyster dredge on the *Mary Amelia*. The dredge is effectively a bag made of steel rings that are dragged along the bed of the river, when the smack is moving slowly sideways on the tide. At the top of this Tollesbury dredge is stamped CK 212, *William & Emily's* number. There is a 'heel' on the dredge so that it can be 'docked' on the rail to let the mud drain out before putting it on the deck to sort the contents.

In the Victorian period sailing smacks with hand dredges were the backbone of a huge oyster industry in Essex and Kent, while some Suffolk rivers had small oyster fisheries. After farming, oysters were the largest industry on the Essex coast. In the 1870s it was claimed that some 300 smacks dredged the Blackwater Estuary, while in 1908 there were some 86 smacks and the steam dredger *Pyefleet* owned on the River Colne.

The demand for oysters tailed off and the hard winters of 1940, 1947 and 1963 all but wiped out the Native oyster stocks. The introduction of quick growing Pacific 'Rock' oysters and a fresh approach to marketing recreated a demand for oysters. Christopher Kerrison's Colchester Oyster Fishery had their sheds on Peewit Island, up Pyefleet, the creek at the back of Mersea Island, that was two miles to the landing at Brightlingsea. In 1981, to revive the Colchester fishery, a new French-style oyster store and shop was built at North Farm at East Mersea beside Pyefleet. At the other end of the island Mersea oysterman Richard Haward opened the Company Shed at West Mersea as a shellfish restaurant and, following on from this, the Tollesbury & Mersea Oyster Company opened another shellfish restaurant on the Coast Road.

The Whitstable smacks 44ft *Thistle*, 41ft *Gamecock* and 40ft *Stormy Petrel* about to sail out of Whitstable harbour for the first Whitstable Oyster Dredging Match in 2003.

The seas funnel into the tiny man-made harbour at Whitstable and in a gale the smacks often put to sea and anchored off the town for safety. The anchorage is slightly protected from the open Thames Estuary by a spit known as the Whitstable Street. In order to survive rolling about at sea the Whitstable smacks were more robust than their fine lined counterparts in Essex. The 41ft smack, *Gamecock*, was built by Collar at Whitstable in 1906, and bought in 1962 by Bill Coleman, who restored her for part-time oyster-dredging under sail. Bill worked the *Gamecock* with the tides, going down to Herne Bay one weekend and towards the 'Ferry House' at Harty the next. The smack lay in the traditional anchorage off the harbour, but was twice run down and sunk by power craft.

The Whitstable smacks *Stormy Petrel* and *Thistle* dredging oysters off Whitstable, 2003.

Geoff Gransden's smack *Thistle*, dredging oysters under sail off Whitstable. The flats off Whitstable dry out at low tide and to try and stop oyster poaching the companies put posts around the layings.

The crews of the smacks and bawleys ashore for the prize-giving of the Oyster Dredging Match on The Packing Marsh Island, West Mersea. The Packing Shed, which is on stilts, was built on a saltings island between Thorn Fleet and Mersea Fleet. In the 1920s oysters were stored here in two sheds ready for collection by a ketch that used to come from France.

Left to right: The smacks *Ethel Alice*, *Dorothy*, *Boadicea* (always pronounced the old way), *Mayflower*, counter-sterned *Mary* and the *Kate* on their moorings in the Besom, West Mersea, 2005. The name Besom for this creek is a corruption of 'broom', once used as withies to mark the channel, leading out into the Blackwater Estuary.

The 36ft *Harriet Blanche* running into the River Colne past Mersea Stone in the 2006 Colne Smack Race. This was her first race after being totally rebuilt at Oare Creek in Kent. The *Harriet Blanche* was built in 1912 by Aldous at Brightlingsea. Aldous built most of the Colne and Blackwater smacks and they all had a similar appearance, but each one was different, being built to its owner's instruction. It was Aldous' practice to put cement in the smacks' bilges. This made them easier to clear out and stopped rot, but when the smacks grew older, the frames rotted just above the cement. The 36ft *Yet*, built in 1898 by Aldous, had about 3 tons of cement in her for ballast. Sometimes metal punchings out of steel plates, to make holes for the rivets, were added to the cement for weight.

The smacks and bawleys laying at Rowhedge after the 2005 annual Smack Race. Rowhedge and Wivenhoe were the principal Colne fishing ports until the railway reached Brightlingsea in 1866 (closed in 1964) and then most smacks operated from this port, near the Colne mouth. Although these smacks mostly have CK registration, and are known as Colchester smacks, none of them used to go up the River Colne to this town.

The first record of a race for fishing smacks in Essex was at Bradwell in 1783 and racing became very popular. In the Victorian and Edwardian eras most of the fishing villages had at least one annual smack race. The rules of the Wivenhoe Smack Race in 1897 show that they were highly regulated events, no doubt the result of many disputes over the years.

In the 1920s most of the smacks had low-powered engines fitted and the races petered out. In 1947 the smack race was revived at West Mersea, the race at Maldon was revived in 1956 and at Brightlingsea an event was restarted in 1972. Racing proved to be a double-edged sword; inspiring people to restore smacks, but eventually the burning passion to win encouraged people to 'develop' their smacks with larger sail areas and very yachty fittings. The desire to get more speed out of the hulls resulted in some smacks looking like racing yachts. By about 2003 The Sailing Smack Association began highly contentious discussions to try and persuade owners to retain the traditional appearance of their smacks.

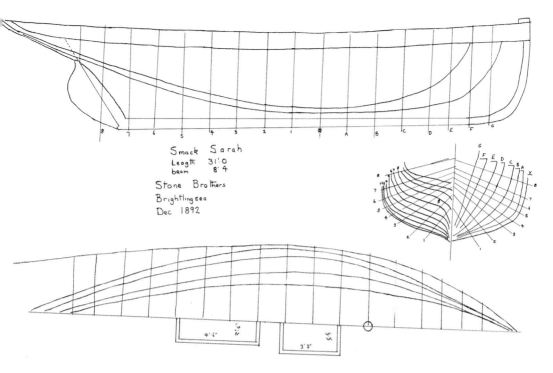

Smack Sarah
Length 31'0
beam 8'4

Stone Brothers
Brightlingsea
Dec 1892

The *Sarah* was a classic Essex smack built at Rowhedge and was 32.6ft from stem to rudder-post, but after being rebuilt by Stone Brothers at Brightlingsea she became 33.6ft. In 1909 the *Sarah* was owned at Tollesbury and skippered by William Myall and was transferred to the Maldon register in 1934. Most barge and smack measurements change when they get rebuilt or even have major repairs.

The 36ft Colchester-registered smack *Primrose* shows the advantage of the long counter stern that increases her waterline length and speed in a strong wind. The smacks were so similar to the Victorian yachts that it was a chicken and egg situation. However, the smacks definitely came first, but because both were built in the same Colneside yards their design was strongly influenced by the great Victorian racing yachts, but retained more practical sail plans.

The 32ft *Electron* was one of the smaller Colchester smacks and was probably intended to just work in the rivers and creeks. Although the hold has been converted to a cabin she has the classic deck layout of an Essex smack. It is an East Coast tradition that jibs and tops'l are white and foresails and mainsails are tanned brown. On the barges the jib and jibtops'ls are left white.

The 40ft *Martha II* and 44ft stowboating smack *Sallie* racing during the Heybridge Basin Regatta, 2005. The *Sallie*, when owned at Tollesbury, went shrimping in the summers off the Suffolk coast from Harwich. At Harwich fishermen watched the warships being 'coaled', when anchored in the River Stour, and when some was spilt the Essex smackmen dredged up the coal and sold it.

'Alfa' Pitt on his 35ft smack *Skylark*, which he had worked single handed, at Bath Wall beach, Maldon, where the smacks always berthed, in about 1955. The Pitts were formerly fishermen at Greenhithe and the Emmetts at Erith, but due to pollution in the Thames they had loaded their furniture on to their smacks and sailed around to settle at Maldon.

The Maldon smacks retained their transom sterns, but in the 1920s 32ft *William* and 33ft *Polly* were given counter sterns, which gave more deck space, and a longer boom, doing away with the topmast.

When fishing in the Blackwater was poor the Maldon smacks were taken fishing and dredging in other Essex rivers. The fishermen lived aboard the smacks and laid Peter nets across the creeks and in the Dengie outfalls. In the winter they towed their 12ft boats and punts astern and went off wildfowling, often being paid to take parties of 'toffs' gunning.

In the 1950s the Essex fishermen were working smacks, which had been built for their grandfathers. Most of these smacks were fitted with engines, but the Maldon smacks, because they worked in the sheltered waters of their estuary, were the last East Coast smacks to work under sail.

Because Maldon dries out at low water the Maldon smacks had to go fishing down-river when there was high water at midday. The following week the smacks left on the early morning tide and returned on the evening tide.

The last Maldon smack working under sail only was the *Polly*, until 1956. That year one of her elderly owners was knocked overboard by the boom and 85 year-old Ernie Pitt said 'we got rid of the little smack afore she got rid of us.' Although fitted with old car engines, the *Skylark* and the Claydon Brothers' 30ft 5ins *Joseph T* were still using sail in 1958. Often they motored downriver and then dredged back under sail. Some Maldon fishermen leased oysters grounds down the river, but it is said they spent so much time raiding each other's grounds that they all ended up with the same amount. At night a raid on Tollesbury and Mersea Company's grounds often proved fruitful.

The 77ft x 19ft 2ins x 5ft 8ins Lowestoft trawling smack *Excelsior* is one of the most authentically restored smacks on the East Coast. She was built by Chambers at Lowestoft in 1921 to replace a smack of the same name lost during World War I. Lowestoft had two fishing communities. The trawler men worked all the year round in the North Sea, and the men on the drifters mainly worked in the 'Great East Anglian herring fishing voyage' in the autumn. Many of the drifter men worked on the farms or on longshore fishing boats for the remainder of the year.

Chapter Five

BAWLEYS AND LEIGH COCKLERS Loose-footed mains'ls

Lucy Harris sailing the *Marigold*. The 29ft 5ins x 11ft clinker-built bawley *Marigold* was built by David Patient at Maldon in 1981 on the lines of his 1869 Gravesend bawley *Lilian*. The original Thames fishing boats were the clinker double-ended peter boats, but in the nineteenth century fishermen needed a more seaworthy craft to work in the open Thames Estuary, so they developed the transom-sterned bawleys.

In order to land good quality shrimp they had to be boiled as soon as they came out of the water and to achieve this they were cooked aboard in a copper. To prevent the boiling water from being spilt the bawleys were given a generous beam for stability. The term bawley was a corruption of 'boiler boat.'

The Leigh bawley *Bona* and the steel barge *Repertor*. The 36ft 10ins x 12ft 11ins *Bona* was built by Aldous at Brightlingsea in 1903. The bawleys were usually built in the same yards as the barges so the two types had much in common. The loose-footed gaff mainsail of the bawley and the spritsail of the barge allowed them to reduce sail quickly and control their speed in confined waters.

Jim Lawrence putting his 34ft 5ins bawley *Saxonia* on the Hard at Brightlingsea. The *Saxonia*, built in 1932 by Aldous at Brightlingsea, was owned by Youngs of Leigh and used for whitebaiting in the Thames mouth from Holehaven or Leigh.

The 34ft x 11ft Leigh cockler *Mary Amelia* with her jackyard topsail set. The *Mary Amelia* was built for the three Osborne Bros in 1914 at Southend. To launch her the builder, Heywood, had her towed down on to the sands by a traction engine, where she floated on the next tide. The cocklers were almost flat-bottomed and had centreboards because they went out and ran aground on the sandbanks, mostly the Maplins. When the tide went down the crew hand raked the cockles and tipped them into the hold. They then waited for the tide to return. The *Mary Amelia* loaded 365 baskets (7 tons) of cockles and if they didn't fill the hold on one tide they slept in the tiny forepeak and worked on the night tide, by lamplight.

Robert Simper on the *Mary Amelia* rounding the end of Southend Pier shortly before the pier was very badly damaged by fire, 2005. The *Mary Amelia* has been given a centreboard winch and windlass, but when working, this cockler had a crew of seven men and there was enough manpower to do the hauling by hand.

Trevor Osborne on the *Mary Amelia*, his grandfather's cockler, with the cockle rake and net they had used to scoop cockles up into baskets. Trevor worked for seven years hand-raking cockles before suction dredgers were introduced. In 2006, he was operating his cockle suction dredger *Renown IV* from the creek at Old Leigh with his son.

Cockles were originally raked up on the foreshore, but in 1810 the building contractor Thomas Hills settled in Leigh and saw an opening to develop a cockle industry. He financed the local men to buy boats to go down to the Maplin Sands and started shipping cockles up to Billingsgate.

The coal-burning stove in the forepeak of the *Mary Amelia*. George Osborne, who began cockling on the *Mary Amelia* in the 1920s, recalled that after four men had hand-raked and loaded 7 tons of cockles they were glad for the warmth of the 'monkey' stove as they slept while waiting for the tide to 'fleet'(float) the boat. The stove always had a pot of stewing tea on it and there was condensed milk in a cupboard.

George recalled that as a boy it was part of his job to walk along the tideline and pick up driftwood for the fire. Barges used to rely on coal 'obtained' from the coal lighters laying in the Thames. Barges only sailed with a favourable tide and anchored or moored to a buoy with a foul tide. The trick was to drop alongside a Cory coal lighter just as it was getting dark, as the river police could not be on patrol all night!

The Leigh shrimper, *Reminder*, at Wivenhoe in 2005. In the 1920s the Leigh men fitted engines into their sailing bawleys, but their deep drafts were a drawback when working up shallow channels. The new generation of shoal draft, motor shrimpers was built, with boilers to cook the shrimp on the way home. These included the 24ft *Girl Pat*, the Meddle's 30ft *Reminder* built by Cole &Wiggins in 1938 and the 28ft *Victorious* in 1945.

On 23 April, 2005, St George's Day, the totally rebuilt 36ft x 11ft 6ins x draft 3ft 6ins cockler *Endeavour*, built in 1924 at Leigh, was re-christened at the Strand Wharf, Leigh-on-Sea. The Endeavour Trust, thanks to support from the Heritage Lottery Fund, had the *Endeavour* totally rebuilt by Brian Kennell and Shaun White, with sails made by Steve Hall, as a memorial to the men lost at Dunkirk.

In 1940 six Leigh cocklers went to the Dunkirk Evacuation and took about 1000 soldiers off the mole to ships, to be ferried back to England. On the return trip Osborne's *Renown* was blow up by a mine, killing three Leigh men and one Naval rating. The Dunkirk veteran Frank Grove, centre, was brought back on one of the Leigh cocklers.

The Leigh cockler *Endeavour*, sailing. In the inter-war years the Leigh men had motor sailers built with centre-boards for cockling. The *Endeavour* was one of those with a low-powered engine, but still had a small sail plan. The *Endeavour* was a successful cockler because the whole hull floated at the same level while the old sailing cocklers often got stuck on the heel, under the stern. Sometimes they had to wait for the next tide before they could get away.

After World War II another series of wooden motor cocklers was built, such as the 43ft *Theodore*, built in 1946, the 40ft *Navigator* in 1948 and the *Renown*. These were still grounded on the banks to hand-rake cockles. However, these motor cocklers proved too big for working on the sands as the *Renown* took an hour and a half longer to float than the pre-war cocklers, like *Endeavour*, thus they lost an hour's working time on each tide.

The larger cocklers had a crew of up to twelve men, and they passed away their time, to and from the cockle grounds, playing cards. Sometimes, if the men lost their share of the days cockles, they would jump off at the first bend so that they didn't have the heavy work of unloading the cockles into baskets with yokes.

The post-war period was the 'Klondyke' years at Leigh when a great deal of money was earned dredging up 'white weed', seaweed used as decorations. The white weeding boom took Leigh to a new peak when in 1951 there were 52 boats and 100 men white weeding and 44 boats and 118 men fishing and cockling. The *Endeavour* was used for white weeding, with a 16hp Lister diesel, when she was owned by Joe Deal and she continued shrimping until 1987.

In 1967 the Meddles tried suction-dredging cockles with their wooden *Ranger II* and soon after this the whole fleet was fitted with suction dredgers which meant that they steamed over the banks, rather than run ashore. The old cocklers worked all the year round, but the suction cocklers only work from June until December, three days a week, and are limited to the number of 'baskets' they can take, per day.

Steve Meddle's brand new suction cockler *Boy Michael*, which can load about 10 tonnes of cockles in an hour and a half, and the sailing cocklers *Alice & Florrie* and *Mary Amelia* on Victoria Wharf, Old Leigh, 2006. At Leigh the fishing fleet is thriving and continuing to develop, but the eight cocklers working on the inner Thames Estuary are restricted as to when they can work.

In 1987 the 44ft steel *Liberator* was the first of new series of steel flat-bottomed suction dredgers operating from Leigh. By 2005 there were eight cocklers, about six trawlers and two white weeders based at Leigh. Two of the cocklers were owned in Boston and their cockles were being taken back to Boston by lorry. Most of the cockles were boiled in a shed at the top of the creek. In 2006 the Common Grounds in the outer estuary on Buxey and Gunfleet were open for just two days and fourteen King's Lynn and then Boston cocklers came around just to work them.

The artist John Cotgrove of Leigh-on-Sea has completely immersed himself in the past of south Essex and recreated the era of working sail on canvas. The golden age of coastal sailing craft, before 1914, has left a powerful imprint on the folk memory of the East Coast of England.

Chapter Six

OPEN BOATS Pulling and sailing boats

A wildfowler in a 'gunning punt' manoeuvring on the River Deben, February, 2005. These flat-bottomed punts are paddled quietly up the rivers during the winter in the hope of getting near large flocks of wildfowl sitting on the water. The gun punt was a Victorian invention used by fishermen to earn a living during a hard winter and by gentlemen for sport shooting. In the 1990s punt gunning became very un-politically correct and was a kind of 'black art', with its participants keeping very quiet about their activities. Walter Linnet, the wildfowler who lived at Bradwell, in the lonely cottage near St. Peter's Chapel, told a young man who was out on the saltings with a gun "boy if you got a pound in your pocket you don't need to shoot the duck.'

The flat-bottomed Manningtree doble can float in a few inches of water and skim over the mud flats in very shallow water in the upper reaches of the River Stour. In 2007 Jim Pittock and 'Long John' Cronin were the last people using dobles for eeling, with Fyke nets. John Cronin built his own small smoke house.

Two duck punts at the Shipways, Maldon, just below John Howard's home and design office. Howard designed the 30ft 7ins x 9ft 3.7ins centreboard yacht *Eider Duck*, built just down the river by Cook & Woodward in 1900. The *Eider Duck* carried two punt guns on her deck and used to anchor near the wildfowl. The gentlemen gunners would then go after the duck and geese in the punts.

Every builder produced his own version of a gunning punt but they always had a 'rocker' bottom. This gave them a slightly banana shape because an entirely flat bottom could create suction in the mud. The flat bottom on a full-sized barge, particularly if loaded, could also create suction and it would fail to rise with the tide. The usual way to break the suction was to run a chain under the bottom.

Les Lucas at the finish of a duck punt race at Manningtree in 1985. Many gunning punts had a small sail and in the summer they were keenly raced at regattas. Although they gave up punt gunning in the 1980s the Lucas family still race punts at Manningtree, but use much lighter ones than the punts used by the old gunners. The punt's original sail was a jacket hung up on an oar to get home, but they are now spritsail and steered with just an oar put over the lee side. For eel fishing and netting for flat fish in numerous creeks leading off the River Stour, the Manningtree men used a flat-bottomed double-ended punt known as a peter boat.

The old gunners had hard times trying to earn some cash out on the wide shallow Stour in a hard winter. One of their chief markets was the Garrison at Colchester. When they couldn't get a goose, one of the plucked Mistley swans had to fill the order.

The 12ft x 3ft 1in x 1ft 4ins mid-Victorian *Teddy* was built by William Garrard & Son in a big shed at the bottom of Brook Street in Woodbridge in 1877 as a fast rowing boat to operate in shallow water. The Woodbridge pilot Sam Marsh had to row her two miles down the River Deben, to the Rocks Reach below Waldringfield to meet sailing barges coming up. The pilots used to go up to the high ground on the Ipswich Road and with a telescope could, before the trees were planted, see a barges tops'l coming in over the Deben Bar.

Barges finished trading into the River Deben in about 1930 and the *Teddy* was then used for eel fishing. In about 1950 Frank Knights put her into a cellar in a Ferry Quay warehouse and she stayed there for over fifty years.

Lawrence Hebson pushing a new plank into place while restoring the *Teddy*. This plank had been steamed for half an hour to allow it to bend. The guideline in restoring the *Teddy* was that as little new wood as possible was to be used and it had to be rebuilt in the original fashion. When built, the hull had an oak keel made of one piece of wood and elm planking. However, the planks were replaced with larch because of the shortage of elm caused by Dutch elm disease.

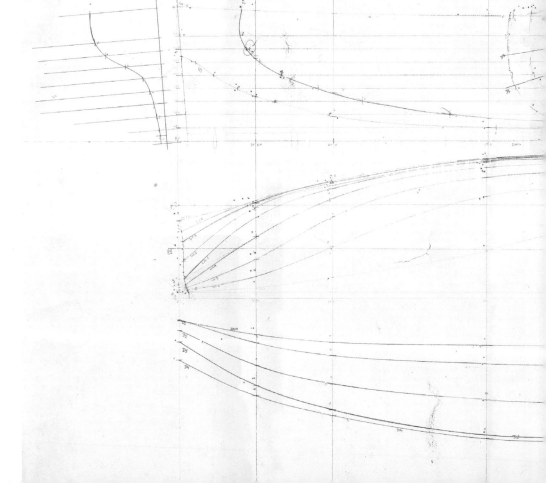

Left: A replica of the *Teddy* being built, larch planks on oak frame, at the International Boat Building Training Centre at Lowestoft.

Plans of the 12ft Woodbridge pilot's boat *Teddy* drawn by the International Boat Building Training Centre, Lowestoft.

The sailing barge *Dawn*, with her barge boat astern, on her way up to the East Mill, Colchester. The boat was a vital part of the barge's gear. In docks it was used to run out mooring ropes and the dolly line, for hauling the barge around. Because they were used in confined waters the boat was usually sculled with an oar over the stern and only rowed in the open estuaries for trips ashore.

The smaller river barges had 12ft 6ins boats, while the larger barges had 14ft boats. The coasting barges, which came under the Board of Trade regulations, had to have buoyancy tanks fitted, bilge grabs and lifelines around the topsides.

Like all workboats, the barge's boats varied a little according to who built them, but they all had to be small enough to be swung inboard between the davits when against wharves. They all had heart-shaped transom sterns with a notch for a sculling oar and a 'fore sheets' deck in the bow for the bargemen to step down on. The boat, often with a lugsail, was also used for 'ship visits' during the days, and sometimes weeks, when barges lay at anchor 'windbound' waiting for favourable weather to make a passage along the coast. Once engines were fitted in barges such delays became less frequent and the boat often just sat on the hatches for months without being used.

Sailmaker Steve Hall with a Tollesbury lobster hoop net in a smack's boat. The hoops were baited and used to catch lobster and there was a larger version to catch fish. The hoop nets were laid on the bottom of the sea with bait in them and the fishermen jerked them up before the lobster could get out.

On a calm day at sea, in 1953, we met the elderly fisherman 'Jockey' Hunt off Bawdsey, working hoop nets near the Cutler Bank. Jockey was about to row some two miles back to Felixstowe Ferry, as no doubt he had done many times before, but was very glad of a tow. He was in a Felixstowe Ferry lobster-boat, a heavy open clinker boat of around 14ft. The pilots had also used this type of boat. Originally the lobster boats had a mast in the centre thwart and when going on a fresh tack the lugsail was dropped; the mast was lifted out, the sail pushed across to the new leeward side and the mast re-stepped and the sail hoisted. The boats at Felixstowe Ferry, East Lane and Shingle Street were the only ones that had their sails shift in this way.

The smack's boat *Musset* at the Aldous Heritage Smack Dock, Brightlingsea with barge *Edme* being towed past. The Tollesbury smack boats were normally 13ft long, but Walter and Keith Musset had this 12ft boat built in about 1954 to make her lighter to haul up the beach, however it made her too short for two men to row.

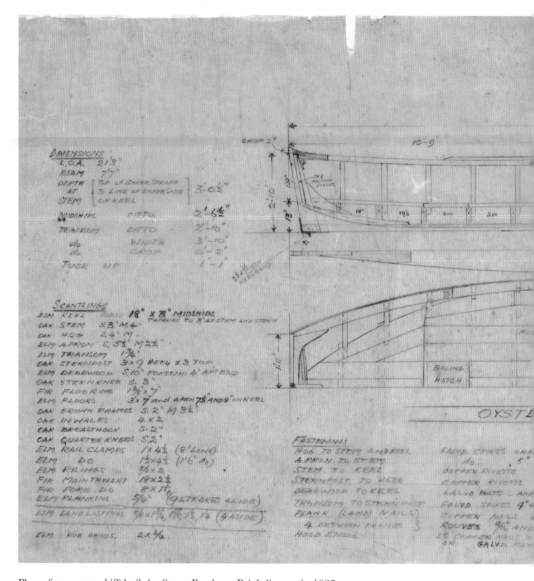

Plan of an oyster skiff built by Stone Brothers, Brightlingsea in 1927.

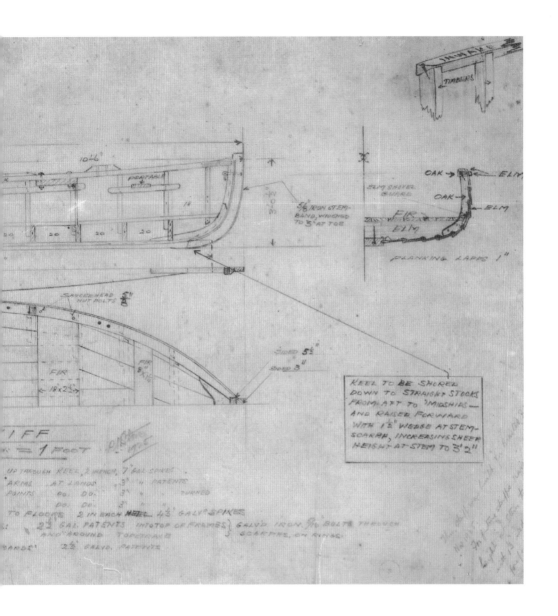

A 12ft 'hack boat' with a notch in the stern for a single oar to be used sculling. This was one of twelve boats built by Aldous in 1942 for the Admiralty, and is typical of the general hack boats of the East Coast. It was said that a barge's boat had bluff bows because it was towed from high up, but a smack's boat had finer bows because it was towed from low down.

The 19ft skiff *Boy George* dredging oysters in the Mersea Dredging Match, 2002. The 'Merseamen' had originally used 'haul and tow skiffs' for working the oyster layings in very narrow creeks. These heavy 20ft clinker-built skiffs, with grown frames, had pointed sterns 'two ended'. This was because they were hauled up and down a creek by a windlass between two anchors with a dredge astern.

At Brightlingsea there was no proper landing place for the smacks so most of the time the sprat and oysters had to be sculled ashore in transom-sterned skiffs. These skiffs had to be good carrying boats and a typical 19 x 8ft skiff, later named the *Toad*, used to carry three and a half tons of sprat. The *Toad* has a 1.4ft wide 'mud keel,' a local feature so that the boats could be pushed down over the mud without sinking in.

The Pulham's Kirby-built skiff *Gypsy* was fitted with an engine during the 1930s, but they only used it to go out to their oyster layings and then dredge under sail, until one windless day they realized that the engine could be kept running for dredging!

The motor skiff *Native Oyster*, built in 1938, was the last of this type of boat worked. William Baker used her on his oyster 'layings' in Salcott Creek until 2002.

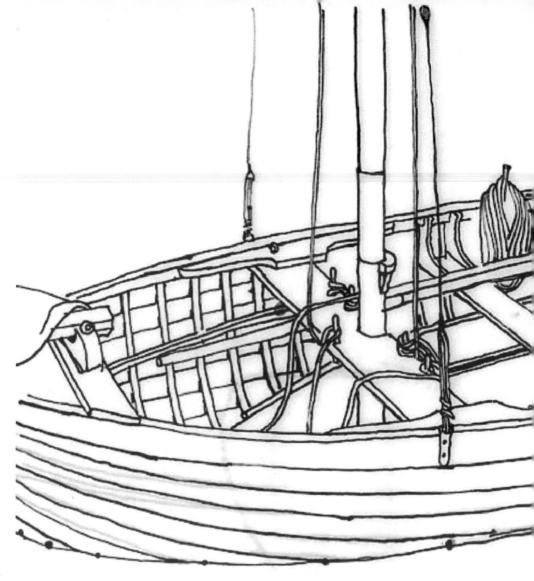

Janet Harker's drawing of her winkle brig *Joy*. The *Joy* was originally the barge's boat for the barge of the same name and David Green converted her for pleasure sailing. The *Joy* was built by Alf Last, who built clinker boats in a shed behind the main buildings at Cooks, Maldon. Alf had started work at Cooks when he left school and promised he would be told if he was going to be taken on permanently. He retired after building the 15ft winkle brigs *Mary Agnes* and then *Prudence* in 1973, but said he had never been told whether he had got the job permanently.

About 1910, Kirby of Brightlingsea started to build 17-20ft clinker open gaff sloops with steamed frames for winkling on the Dengie Flats and summer 'tripping'. The assortment of open boats at West Mersea and on the River Colne were often referred to as being 'poor man's smacks.'

By the 1950's the term 'winkle brig' was used at West Mersea for an open gaff boat sailed for pleasure. So many winkle brigs, skiffs and other clinker craft have been rigged out to race that the West Mersea Open Fishing Boat Association was formed to regulate racing and attempt to prevent them from being developed away from the traditional workboats.

The West Mersea winkle brig *Jack* fitted out for racing. These boats were open, without a thwart amidships, so that they could be used for dredging. The winkle brigs had steamed frames, which made them strong enough to carry the heavy weight when transporting oysters.

Winkle brigs racing in the River Blackwater, 1996.

Janet Harker and her son Ben Light sailing the *Charles Harker* at the official naming of the boat, at Brightlingsea in 2006. Charles Harker, who was dedicated to keeping local traditional boats sailing, had been chairman of the Pioneer Trust and they decided to name the *Pioneer's* boat in his memory.

The hull is a glass-fibre copy from the mould of the *Northdown's* traditional 14ft barge's boat, built by shipwright Alf Last in 1971 at Walter Cook & Son, Hythe, Maldon. A traditionally shaped hull lives on in a new material.

Fishermen shaking herring out of a drift net on Shingle Street beach in about 1930. At the time there were five boats working off the Shingle Street beach and the children used to race home from school to help walk around the capstan bars as the boats were dragged up the beach.

The shingle ridge between the Oxley Marshes and Hollesley Bay was settled because it was of no use for grazing and no-one bothered about land ownership. The original houses at Shingle Street were just low wooden cottages, built from wood that had been washed ashore, either from ships wrecked on the Ness or from deck cargoes that had broken loose. The men picked up a living piloting, fishing and loading barges with shingle. By the 1920s tourism had already begun with people coming to take their holidays here and during the summer the fishing families rented out their cottages and moved into sheds at the back.

The steep beach in front of the German Ocean Mansion and the Coastguard Cottages at Shingle Street in about 1967. Ron Harris' boats are the nearest and Eric Andrews' boat is over near the Coastguard Cottages. The last sailing boat was the *Snowdrop* and the first motorboat built for Shingle Street was Charles Lucock's *Lassie* in 1924, and named after his dog. When, in about 1938, Eric Andrews wanted a new pilot boat he had Eversons of Woodbridge build the *Gem*, which was the last Suffolk boat built with a mast in the centre thwart, so that it could be lifted out when tacking to push the sail over, and had clips inside the bow to attach to the leading edge of the lugsail.

In 1940 Shingle Street was evacuated and used for a practice bombing range. From the high ground at Hollesley some Shingle Street people watched the bombs hit and destroy the 'Lifeboat Inn' and the next-door fishermen's sheds with all their gear in it. After World War II the hamlet was rebuilt, but men only worked part time from here. The last one was James Green who, in about 1985, bought the Thorpeness boat *Our Soles* and attempted to revive fishing. He trawled for sole in 'The Bay' (Hollesley Bay) and went outside the Cutler Bank to longline for dogfish.

In the 1953 Floods, Shingle Street became an island. The Rev Will Groom rowed out with stores from Hollesley village shop. While the Post woman arranged for two Borstal Boys to row her out. The marshes had been flooded before, in 1906, when the sea broke through the shingle on the Bawdsey side of Shingle Street and a barge was towed around from Ipswich and sunk in the gap.

In 2007 94-year-old Nina Harris remembered Shingle Street as a fishing hamlet. Her great-grandfather E. Norton was captain of the schooner *Rudolph* when she was wrecked at Shingle Street in 1895. The schooner was arriving from Hartlepool with coal for Orford. The wind was NW by N and only force 2 and presumably the force of the tide swept her ashore at the Ore mouth and the hull became badly strained.

Nina Harris' grandfather had been a Shingle Street fisherman and pilot, bringing yachts and barges into the River Ore, but her father kept the 'Three Mariners' at Slaughden Quay, Aldeburgh. She was born there in 1912, but the Nortons had returned to Shingle Street before the public house and most of Slaughden went into the sea. At least one Aldeburgh fishermen used to fish over the site of the Slaughden house where he had been born.

Nina Harris, after a long lifetime of living within the sound of the sea, was undaunted by the dangers, saying 'Tides come up and tides go down.'

Vic Smith's Aldeburgh boat going off trawling, in the 1930s. The sails are worn and torn, a common situation in the financially difficult inter-war years. The clinker beach boats that work in the longshore fishery off the Suffolk coast are the very end of this long era. In the fourth century the Anglo-Saxons brought the art of clinker boat building to East Anglia, probably from the southern shore of the Baltic, and this type of hull has been in regular use for over fifteen hundred years.

These longshore fishing beach boats were called 'punts' at Southwold and 'boats' around Aldeburgh and were very seaworthy in the short seas of the North Sea. The sailing boats were light enough to be hauled up with 6-man hand capstans, known at Southwold as 'bulls.' The Suffolk boats had wide bows because they were launched down steep shingle beaches and had to rise as they hit the first incoming waves. They were also fine below the waterline so that they could be rowed.

In calm weather an 18ft boat carried three and half tons in the 'fish rooms' amidships and had boards to stop the catch from sliding about. the boats used to be loaded down to just below the top plank and rowed ashore. They worked the tides, when drifting for herring or sprat, so that they finished up just off the beach.

Being able to land safely on an open beach was more important to the fishermen than a fast sailing boat so they were happy with flat bottomed Suffolk longshore boats. They were occasionally swamped when coming ashore on the open beaches and this was looked on as being bad seamanship, although fishermen always went to the aid of anyone in trouble. When engines were first introduced they were taken out during the drifting season to avoid tainting the fish with the smell of the fuel. When trawling in the summer, the Aldeburgh men liked to have a mizzen set to keep the bow pointing up into wind, while the stern was kept 'down to the name' with bags of shingle.

There were boats fishing off Aldeburgh beach in the Elizabethan period and records tell of 300 men returning in the autumn for the 'Spratte Fare.' In the Victorian period 200 men took part in the sprat fishing and when Billy Burrell started fishing in 1940 there were still around 90 men and about 30 boats working from the beach during the sprat fishery. The Aldeburgh fishermen nearly always had other jobs that they could return to for part of the year. Often, in patches of bad weather, they could only get off the beach for a couple of days in a month.

In 1983 there were thirty men, fishing in twenty boats, working off the beach in peak periods, but by 2005 most of the boats had gone and only one boat was 'beach fishing'. However, two more glass-fibre hulled boats returned the following year.

Colin Smith's 22ft *Rachel Linda*, built by Russell Upson at Slaughden Quay in 1980, was the only wooden boat being used for fishing from Aldeburgh beach by 2006.

Dean Fryer fished for twelve years in the wooden clinker-built boat *Jill Ann* that had a speed of 6 knots. In 1996 he bought the 20ft catamaran *Excel* and her 28-knot speed allowed him to work lobster pots, lines and nets all in the same day. In 2006 he bought the larger catamaran *Enterprise*, but instead of being hauled up the beach by a winch, she was brought up on a trailer.

Mostly these boats worked close to the beach, trawling in The Garden just off the shore. John Harling remembers in the 1970s the furthest they went out was eight miles to the Shipwash, longlining for cod. They would lay out their lines and then go aboard the Shipwash light-vessel to get warm and exchanged fish and newspapers for cups of tea, made with condensed milk. However, the motion in the cabins of the large light-vessel made them feel sick and they were happy to get back into their open 20ft *Enterprise* and return to hauling their longlines.

To bait their longlines for cod and dogfish the fishermen had 'bait sheds' on or near the beach, mostly at the south end. After the 1953 Floods more sheds were built further up the beach, near the Moot Hall. Until the 1960s much of the catch was sent away by rail, but as catches declined fishermen received extra income from retailing straight to the public from the Fourteen Fishermen's sheds on the beach. This enabled the Aldeburgh fleet to survive.

Harry Harling on Thorpeness beach about 1900 with his boat *Gypsy Queen*. The Thorpe boats would trawl 'down' the tide to Sizewell Bank and then race back. Harry Harling had a boat for each type of fishing. The 21ft *Gypsy Queen* was for trawling in the summer. The 18ft *Industry* was for driftnet fishing for sprat and herring and the smaller 14ft skiff was for potting, on The Rocks near the shore, for crab and lobster. All these clinker boats were built of oak, the most common tree in Suffolk. From the profits fishing Harry Harling had five houses in Thorpeness and opened the first shop here.

By 1914 fourteen fishermen were working off Thorpeness beach. To drag their boats up the beach the summer visitors, particularly the girls, used to rush down to walk around the capstans. Sometimes when the fishing was poor the fishermen would load their nets, capstans and even a small shed, for oilskins, into their boats and move up to Sizewell. Other times they moved south eleven miles around Orfordness and on to the beach at East Lane, Bawdsey. The larger boat was turned upside-down and they lived under it. The 18ft boat was used for fishing and carried the catch to be sold at Woodbridge or Harwich. Once the Westrups were caught by a gale near Orfordness when moving south and had a bad time. For shelter they ran into 'Aldeburgh Harbour'(mouth of the River Ore) and anchored and lived under the sails until the wind dropped. After this they all stayed on Thorpeness beach.

To make life easier a small railway track was laid from Thorpeness beach up to the road and from here the catch was taken to the station and on to Lowestoft fish market. Harry Harling fitted his first engine, a three and a half hp. Winconsin, in *Gypsy Queen*, in 1914. In the 1953 Floods the fishermen got most of the boats up on to high ground, but one was swept on to the marshes and broken while the 'crab' capstans were buried by 10ft of shingle.

The Thorpeness boat, the 18ft 4ins x 7ft 1in *Three Sisters*, setting an old white fores'l with a light yard that had been made in 1957 for Jim Churchyard's 18ft *Happy Thought*. The *Happy Thought* sank off Aldeburgh in about 1990 and other fishermen rescued the two men aboard.

When the *Three Sisters* was built in 1896, as a sailing beach boat, she was a plank lower, so that she could be rowed. When an engine was fitted the hull was 'rose on' with an extra plank. The extra plank was kept on her hull when rebuilt in 1994. Billy Burrell recalled that in the Aldeburgh Regatta races, off the beach, the narrow-sterned *Three Sisters* was usually hauled back up the beach before the others had finished racing. Percy Westrup fitted an 8hp Stuart Turner petrol in *Three Sisters* and fished with her off Thorpeness until about 1953.

John and Graham Westrup at Thorpeness loading herring nets on a net 'barrow' ready to put aboard their 14ft boat, *Shady Nook*, in 2002. The *Shady Nook* was built by Whisstocks in 1953 for the Thorpeness fisherman Tim Brown and named after his bungalow. The last full time fishermen at Thorpeness and they gave up in the 1950s.

The *Shady Nook*, was typical of the Suffolk beach boats of the 1940-50s which only had a 8hp Stuart Turner petrol engine, but once more powerful diesel engines were available higher sided beamy 'bulldog bow' boats were built. The Westrups bought the glass-fibre *Gill Jan* to fish part-time off Thorpeness in the summer and Southwold in the winter.

The beach skiff *Jumbo* on Dunwich beach in 1979. This boat originally came from Kessingland, Kess'el to the old beachmen, and has raised bow boards fitted because an outboard was being used. The beach skiff was a light rowing boat for working close to the beach in fine weather.

'Dodger' Holmes' 19ft 3ins x 9ft 5ins *Dodger* trawling off the Dingle Marshes, Dunwich in 2001, Frank Knights at Woodbridge launched her in 1991 and she was the last wooden boat built to work off the Suffolk beach. The *Dodger*, when new, had joined five other boats fishing off Dunwich beach.

Steven King's longshore fishing boat *Jill Anne* was the only boat left fishing off Dunwich beach in 2006. He fishes in the summer and autumn and goes reed-cutting in the winter.

   The difficulties of landing on an open beach in bad weather meant the Dunwich men lost about 12-16 weeks fishing every year. Although they were only at sea in these open boats for a short while, it was extremely hard work and very physically demanding. The men didn't seem to mind that, it was the lack of fish and falling incomes that caused them to give up.

   Fishermen never leave anything for the boat coming up astern. The problem is that with powerful engines, sophisticated nets and fish-finding equipment they can literally take everything.

A beach capstan at Southwold.

Suffolk beach punt *Alice Maud* running a summer pleasure trip c1905.

Kessingland fishing boats racing.

A Southwold Fisherman shaking sprat out of a drift net on the beach in front of the town.
This records a successful fishing trip, but often-traditional working boats were linked to hardship and poverty.
The Suffolk beach boats lack of a centreboard or keel was the reason for their survival at sea. When caught by
a squall the boat simply blew to leeward instead of capsizing.

NOTES.

NOTES.